# Volume 1

# First Steps in
# Mathematics

## Number

*Improving the mathematics
outcomes of students*

Department of
**Education
and Training**

# Contents

# CHAPTER 1

# What Are the Features of This Resource Book?

The *First Steps in Mathematics: Number* Resource Books will help teachers to diagnose, plan, implement and judge the effectiveness of the teaching and learning experiences they provide for their students. *First Steps in Mathematics: Number* has two Resource Books. The first book examines the outcomes relating to Understand Whole and Decimal Numbers and Understand Fractional Numbers. The second book includes Calculate, Understand Operations and Reason About Number Patterns.

This Resource Book includes the following elements:

- Diagnostic Map
- Mathematics Outcomes
- Levels of Achievement
- Pointers
- Key Understandings
- Sample Learning Activities
- Sample Lessons
- 'Did You Know?' sections.
- Background Notes

# Diagnostic Maps

The purpose of the Diagnostic Maps is to help teachers:

- understand why students seem to be able to do some things and not others

- realise why some students may be experiencing difficulty while others are not

- indicate the challenges students need to move their thinking forward, to refine their preconceptions, overcome any misconceptions, and so achieve the outcomes

- interpret their students' responses to activities.

Each map includes key indications and consequences of students' understanding and growth. This information is crucial for teachers making judgments about their students' level of understanding of mathematics. It enhances teachers' judgments about what to teach, to whom and when to teach it.

## *Using the Diagnostic Maps*

The Diagnostic Maps are intended to assist teachers as they plan their mathematics curriculum. The Diagnostic Maps describe the characteristic phases in the development of students' thinking about the major concepts in each set of outcomes. The descriptions of the phases help teachers make judgments about students' understandings of the mathematical concepts.

The text in the shaded sections of each map describes students' major preoccupations, or focus, during that phase of thinking about the mathematics strand.

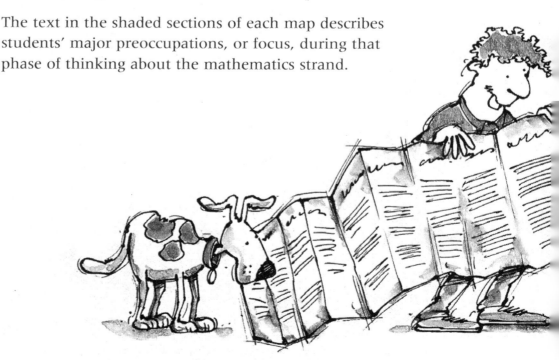

The 'By the end' section of each phase provides examples of what students typically think and are able to do as a result of having worked through the phase.

The achievements in the 'By the end' section should be read in conjunction with the 'As students move from' section. The 'As students move from' section includes the preconceptions, partial conceptions and misconceptions that students may have developed along the way. These provide the learning challenges for the next phase.

Together, the 'By the end' and 'As students move from' sections illustrate that while students might have developed a range of important understandings as they passed through the phase, they might also have developed some unconventional or unhelpful ideas at the same time. Both of these sections of the Diagnostic Map are intended as a useful guide only.

## Mathematics Outcomes

The mathematics outcomes indicate what students are expected to know, understand and be able to do as a result of their learning experiences. The outcomes provide a framework for developing a mathematics curriculum that is taught to particular students in particular contexts. The outcomes for Number are located at the beginning of each section of the two Resource Books.

# Levels of Achievement

There are eight Levels of Achievement for each mathematics outcome. The *First Steps in Mathematics* Resource Books address Levels 1 to 5 of these outcomes because they cover the typical range of achievement in primary school.

The Levels of Achievement describe markers of progress towards full achievement of the outcomes. Each student's achievement in mathematics can be monitored and success judged against the Levels of Achievement.

As the phases of the Diagnostic Maps are developmental, and not age specific, the Levels of Achievement will provide teachers with descriptions of the expected progress that students will make every 18 to 20 months when given access to an appropriate curriculum.

# Pointers

Each Level of Achievement has a series of Pointers. They provide examples of what students might typically do if they have achieved a level. The Pointers help clarify the meaning of the mathematics outcome and the differences between the Levels of Achievement.

# Key Understandings

The Key Understandings are the cornerstone of the *First Steps in Mathematics* series. The Key Understandings:

- describe the mathematical ideas, or concepts, which students need to know in order to achieve the outcome
- explain how these mathematical ideas relate to the levels of achievement for the mathematics outcomes
- suggest what experiences teachers should plan for students so they achieve the outcome
- provide a basis for the recognition and assessment of what students already know and still need to know in order to progress
- indicate the emphasis of the curriculum at particular stages
- provide content and pedagogic advice to assist with planning the curriculum at the classroom and whole-school levels.

The number of Key Understandings for each mathematics outcome varies according to the number of 'big mathematical ideas' students need to achieve the outcome.

## Sample Learning Activities

For each Key Understanding, there are Sample Learning Activities that teachers could use to develop the mathematical ideas of the Key Understanding. The activities are organised into three broad groups.

- Beginning activities are suitable for Kindergarten to Year 3 students.
- Middle activities cater for Year 3 to Year 5 students.
- Later activities are designed for Year 5 to Year 7 students.

If students in the later years have not had enough prior experience, then teachers may need to select and adapt activities from earlier groups.

## Sample Lessons

The Sample Lessons illustrate some of the ways in which teachers can use the Learning Activities for the Beginning, Middle and Later groups. The emphasis is on how teachers can focus students' attention on the mathematics during the learning activity.

## 'Did You Know?' Sections

For some of the Key Understandings, there are 'Did You Know?' sections. These sections highlight common understandings and misunderstandings that students have. Some 'Did You Know?' sections also suggest diagnostic activities that teachers may wish to try with their students.

## Background Notes

The Background Notes supplement the information provided in the Key Understandings. These notes are designed to help teachers develop a more in-depth knowledge of what is required as students achieve the mathematics outcomes.

The Background Notes are based on extensive research and are more detailed than the descriptions of the mathematical ideas in the Key Undertandings. The content of the Background Notes varies. Sometimes, they describe how students learn specific mathematical ideas. Other notes explain the mathematics of some outcomes that may be new or unfamiliar to teachers.

# CHAPTER 2

# The Number Outcomes

The Number strand focuses on numbers and operations—what they mean, how we represent them, and how and why we use them in our everyday lives. As a result of their learning, students will develop a good sense of numbers and operations and the relationships between them. Students will develop confidence in their ability to deal with numerical situations with flexibility, ease and efficiency.

To achieve this, students require a sound grasp of the meanings of numbers and how we write them. They also need to develop an understanding of the meaning and use of basic operations, a working and flexible repertoire of computational skills, and the capacity to identify and work with number patterns and relationships. A wide range of learning experiences will enable students to understand numbers, understand operations, and to calculate and reason about number patterns and relationships.

As a result they will be should be able to achieve the following outcomes.

### Understand Whole and Decimal Numbers

Read, write and understand the meaning, order and relative magnitudes of whole and decimal numbers, moving flexibly between equivalent forms.

### Understand Fractional Numbers

Read, write and understand the meaning, order and relative magnitudes of fractional numbers, moving flexibly between equivalent forms.

**Understand Operations**

Understand the meaning, use and connections between addition, multiplication, subtraction and division.

**Calculate**

Choose and use a repertoire of mental, paper and calculator computational strategies for each operation, meeting required degrees of accuracy and judging the reasonableness of results.

**Reason About Number Patterns**

Investigate, generalise and reason about patterns in numbers, explaining and justifying the conclusions reached.

# Integrating the Outcomes

Each mathematics outcome in Number is explored in a separate chapter. This is to emphasise both the importance of each outcome and the differences between them. For example, students need to learn about the meaning, properties and use of addition (Understand Operations) as well as being able to add numbers (Calculate). By paying separate and special attention to each outcome, teachers can make sure that both areas receive sufficient attention, and that the important ideas about each are drawn out of the learning experiences they provide.

This does not mean, however, that the ideas and skills underpinning each of the outcomes should be taught separately, or that they will be learned separately. The outcomes are inextricably linked. Consequently, many of the activities will provide opportunities for students to develop their ideas about more than one of the outcomes. This will help teachers to ensure that the significant mathematical ideas are drawn from the learning activities, so that their students achieve each of the mathematics outcomes for Number.

# A Snapshot of the Levels of Achievement in Number

Students should not always be expected to be at the same level of achievement for each of the outcomes in Number. Students vary, so some may progress more rapidly with several aspects of Number than others. Teaching and learning programs also vary and may, at times, inadvertently or deliberately emphasise some aspects of Number more than others.

Nevertheless, while the outcomes for Number are dealt with separately in these materials, they should be developing together and supporting each other, leading to an integrated set of concepts within students' heads.

The levels for each mathematics outcome indicate the typical things students are expected to do at the same time. Generally, students who have access to a curriculum that deals appropriately and thoroughly with each of the outcomes reach a particular level at roughly the same time for each outcome in Number.

> *A student has achieved a level of a **particular outcome** when he or she is able to do all the things described at that level consistently and autonomously over the range of common contexts or experiences.*

> *A student has achieved a level of a **set of outcomes** when he or she consistently and autonomously produces work of the standard described over the full range of outcomes at that level.*

Judgment will be needed to decide whether a student has achieved a particular level. When mapping and reporting a student's long-term progress, a teacher has to find the specific outcome level or the level for the set of outcomes that best fits the student, in the knowledge that no description is likely to fit perfectly.

The Level Statements for Number are on pages 156 to 168.

# CHAPTER 3

# Understand Whole and Decimal Numbers

This chapter will support teachers in developing teaching and learning programs that relate to this outcome:

> *Read, write and understand the meaning, order and relative magnitudes of whole and decimal numbers, moving flexibly between equivalent forms.*

## *Overall Description*

Students read, write, say, interpret and use numbers in common use, including whole numbers, fractions, decimals, percentages and negative numbers.

Students can order numbers and understand the relevance of the order. For example, students know that if one collection has nine items and another has seven, they do not have to line up the items to say which collection has more. Students also know that: cordial that is one-quarter concentrate will be stronger than cordial that is one-fifth concentrate; a library book with call number 7.52 is located after a book with call number 7.513; and a temperature of −16°C is colder than −3°C.

Students understand the relative magnitudes of numbers; for example, nine is always two more than seven, '30% off' is not quite as good as 'one third off', and one million is one thousand times as big as 1000.

Students choose forms of numbers that are helpful in particular contexts. They recognise common equivalences, such as one fifth is the same as $\frac{1}{5}$, two tenths, 0.2 and 20%. Students interpret large and small numbers for which few visual or concrete references are available, and they represent them with scientific notation if appropriate. Students' number repertoire includes irrational numbers, such as 1, and those numbers that arise in practical contexts.

| Levels of Achievement | Pointers<br>Progress will be evident when students: | |
|---|---|---|
| Students have achieved Level 1 when they read, write and say small whole numbers, using them to say how many things there are, make collections of a given size and describe order. | • match oral names to written numbers into the teens and write recognisable versions of them<br>• say the number names, in order, into the teens and respect the order when counting<br>• continue the 1 to 9 pattern within a decade (e.g. 31, 32, 33); although some may need help moving, say, from 39 to 40<br>• say how many are in visible collections of objects; e.g. when shown six pebbles, they can answer the question 'How many are there?'<br>• when counting small collections, use the last number said to answer the 'how many' question<br>• make or draw collections of a given size; e.g. respond correctly to 'Give me seven bears.' | • count by adding one each time, beginning with 0 and press ➕ 1️⃣ repeatedly on a calculator or in order to count; e.g. make a calculator that shows 5 change to 6<br>• understand and use 'first', 'second', etc., to indicate position in a sequence; e.g. I put the pink bear third.<br>• sort coins and notes and realise that coins and notes have different values<br>• give one each of a collection to a group of students, then repeat the cycle until all are distributed, and see this as 'fair shares'; e.g. distribute eight sweets among four students |
| Students have achieved Level 2 when they read, write, say and count with whole numbers to beyond 100, using them to compare collection sizes and describe order. | • read, write and say the numbers in order to beyond 100 and count on or back from any number to 100<br>• choose counting as a strategy to produce equivalent collections and to compare collections<br>• recognise counting as a measure of set size and are convinced that they should get the same answer each time regardless of the strategy, the arrangement of the objects, or the order in which the objects are counted | • understand that you can tell from the numbers alone which collection has more<br>• estimate the size of a collection up to 20 by mentally or visually grouping the items, or comparing it with one of a known size<br>• count coins in multiples of 5c, 10c, 20c, 50c, $1 and $2, and record total amounts<br>• read amounts of money and make up the amount with coins in different ways<br>• decide whether or not they have more or less money than the price and whether to expect change |
| Students have achieved Level 3 when they read, write, say and count with whole numbers into the 1000s, money and familiar measurements. | • read and write any whole number into the 1000s<br>• distinguish and order whole numbers<br>• count up and down in 10s from any starting number<br>• produce and use standard partitions of two- and three-digit numbers<br>• produce non-standard partitions of two-digit numbers to assist in computation | • round numbers up or down, or to the nearest 10 or 100<br>• use the decimal point in representing quantities or money<br>• regroup money to the fewest number of notes and coins<br>• enter and read amounts of money on a calculator, truncating calculator displays to the nearest cent or unit |
| Students have achieved Level 4 when they read, write, say, count with and compare whole numbers into the millions and decimals (equal number of places). | • count forwards and backwards from any whole number<br>• use place value to read, write, say and interpret large whole numbers, oral or written<br>• understand the multiplicative nature of the relationship between places for whole numbers<br>• say decimals correctly<br>• use models to present decimals | • explain why money and measures use decimal notation<br>• rewrite a decimal as a fraction<br>• read scales including where each calibration may not be labelled<br>• count in decimal fractions<br>• use the symbols = , < and > to state comparisons |
| Students have achieved Level 5 when they read, write, say and understand the meaning order and relative magnitude of whole and decimal numbers and integers. | • understand the multiplicative relationship between decimal places<br>• use place value to explain why one decimal fraction is bigger or smaller than another<br>• locate whole and decimal numbers on a range of graduated scales including number lines<br>• find a number between two decimals | • partition decimals in standard ways<br>• use place value to partition decimals flexibly<br>• use whole number powers and square roots in describing things<br>• use whole negative numbers to compare and order measures<br>• locate negative integers on a number line |

## Key Understandings

Teachers will need to plan learning experiences that include and develop the following Key Understandings (KU), which underpin achievement of the outcome. The learning experiences should connect to students' current knowledge and understandings rather than to their year level.

| Key Understanding | Stage of Primary Schooling—Major Emphasis | KU Description | Sample Learning Activities |
|---|---|---|---|
| KU1 We can count a collection to find out how many are in it. | Beginning ✔✔✔<br>Middle ✔ | page 12 | Beginning, page 14<br>Middle, page 18 |
| KU2 We can often see how many are in a collection just by looking and also by thinking of it in parts. | Beginning ✔✔✔<br>Middle ✔✔<br>Later ✔✔ | page 24 | Beginning, page 26<br>Middle, page 28<br>Later, page 30 |
| KU3 We can use numbers in ways that do not refer to quantity. | Beginning ✔✔<br>Middle ✔<br>Later ✔ | page 32 | Beginning, page 34<br>Middle, page 36<br>Later, page 38 |
| KU4 The whole numbers are in a particular order, and there are patterns in the way we say them which help us to remember the order. | Beginning ✔✔✔<br>Middle ✔✔<br>Later ✔✔ | page 40 | Beginning, page 42<br>Middle, page 44<br>Later, page 46 |
| KU5 There are patterns in the way we write whole numbers that help us remember their order. | Beginning ✔✔<br>Middle ✔✔✔<br>Later ✔✔✔ | page 52 | Beginning, page 54<br>Middle, page 56<br>Later, page 58 |
| KU6 Place value helps us to think of the same whole number in different ways and this can be useful. | Beginning ✔<br>Middle ✔✔<br>Later ✔✔✔ | page 60 | Beginning, page 62<br>Middle, page 64<br>Later, page 66 |
| KU7 We can extend the patterns in the way we write whole numbers to write decimals. | Beginning ✔<br>Middle ✔✔<br>Later ✔✔✔ | page 68 | Beginning, page 70<br>Middle, page 71<br>Later, page 72 |
| KU8 We can compare and order the numbers themselves. | Beginning ✔<br>Middle ✔✔<br>Later ✔✔✔ | page 74 | Beginning, page 76<br>Middle, page 78<br>Later, page 80 |

**Key**

✔✔✔ The development of this Key Understanding is a major focus of planned activities.

✔✔ The development of this Key Understanding is an important focus of planned activities.

✔ Some activities may be planned to introduce this Key Understanding, to consolidate it, or to extend its application. The idea may also arise incidentally in conversations and routines that occur in the classroom.

## KEY UNDERSTANDING 1

### *We can count a collection to find out how many are in it.*

In everyday use, 'to count' has two meanings. It can mean to recite the whole number names in their right order, beginning at 1 (*I can count to 20. One, two, three, four, …*). It can also mean to check a collection one by one in order to say how many are in it (*I counted and found there were 14 left*). Key Understanding 1 focuses on the latter meaning. The former meaning is an aspect of Key Understanding 4.

The significance of counting is that it enables us to decide how many are in a collection or to make a collection of a given size. However, we can sometimes 'see' how many without actually counting. To be able 'to count' a collection of things, a student must remember the number names in the right order and be able to use them to decide 'how many'. Students will learn to do this in different ways and in different orders, so different sequences and types of learning activities may be needed. The Sample Learning Activities for Key Understanding 1 should help students link the order in which we say the number names with the size of collections.

Students need to internalise the following five principles for counting a collection if they are to fully accept that counting 'works' and must always give the same answer each time.

1. • Each object to be counted must be touched or 'included' exactly once as the numbers are said.

2. • The numbers must be said once and always in the conventional order.

3. • The objects can be touched in any order, and the starting point and order in which the objects are counted does not affect how many there are.

4. • The arrangement of the objects does not affect how many there are.

5. • The last number said tells 'how many' in the whole collection. It does not describe the last object touched.

Students who have achieved Level 1 of the outcome for [*matching*] Understand Numbers understand what it is that they have to do in response to questions or requests, such as: How many dogs are there? Give me seven forks. Students will match the numbers in order as they point to or look at each object exactly once. They know the last number said answers the 'how many' question.

However, many students do not fully understand the five principles listed on the opposite page and so may still think that if they start in a different place, they could get a different answer. They may not fully trust the count and may not choose to count. Thus, students who can count, when they are asked to find 'how many', or if the word 'count' is mentioned, may not trust it to help them decide, for example, if there are enough drinks for other students. They may simply hand out the drinks or put a name to each drink, or guess. Students need to learn to trust the count and, without prompting, to choose 'counting' as a way of solving such problems. Experience with problem situations in which students are not always told to count or to find how many, should help them move from the ~~&~~ Matching phase through to the Quantifying phase.

[*trust the count know how many*]

Students who have achieved Level 2 do trust and use counting for [*Quantifying*] themselves. They know that any collection has only one 'count'. They would laugh at the idea that a collection could have both 26 and 27 objects. To them, it is obvious that you can tell from the numbers alone which collection is bigger, that a collection of 27 objects always has one more than a collection of 26. Until students realise this, they cannot fully understand numbers as abstractions with properties of their own such as 27 is greater than 26.

Students need to learn to use equal groupings or parts to help count large collections. Students who only learn to skip count by reciting every second or every third number, or by jumping along a number line saying, 2, 4, 6, 8, and so on, may not realise that skip counting also tells you 'how many'. These students will need a lot of practical experience in order to see that pulling out three at a time and counting by threes gives the same answer as if they had counted by ones.

Trusting that all the different ways of counting must give the same number is the key to advancing from Level 1 to Level 2 of the mathematics outcome.

# SAMPLE LEARNING ACTIVITIES

## Beginning ✔✔✔

### Birthday Claps

Ask students to clap once for each birthday they have had. Have students link each clap with each number name as it is said.

### Age Groups

Make a classroom display of students' names (photos). Arrange the names (photos) according to age groups. Have students count how many are in each group and then write number labels for the groups (e.g. *8 students are 4 years old. 15 students are 5 years old.*) As each student has a birthday, ask the student to move his or her name (photo) across to the appropriate age group. Invite all students to count how many in each group now. Ask: Which group must get smaller (bigger)?

### Teeth

Vary the 'Birthdays' activity by asking students to count how many in the class have (have not) lost teeth. (See Sample Lesson 1, page 20.)

### Collections

Have students make collections of a given number of things for real tasks; for example, have them choose six beads to make a necklace.

### How Many?

Ask students to read number labels on storage containers to see how many things they have to get. Label shelves to show how many blocks of each type there are in the containers. During 'packing away time', ask students: How many blocks have you returned so far? How many more do we need to find?

### Keeping Fit

Have students decide each day (week) how many jumps and hops to include in their daily fitness routine and then record the number. Ask students to decide whether they need more or less of each action and to record this new number. Ask: How many jumps (hops) will we have today (this week)?

### Labelling Collections

Invite students to count and write number labels for collections they have sorted and graphed, such as shells, into categories of their own choosing. Have them show how they know there are more in one group than another. Ask: How do you know eight is more than seven? Would eight elephants be more than seven elephants?

### Counting Cakes

Have students count a line of objects (e.g. play dough 'cakes'). Ask: Will there be the same number of cakes if we start counting from the other end? Why? Why not? Count the objects again but, this time, start with the middle object. If a student can't do this, repeat with three objects and increase the quantity by one each time. Ask: What did you do to count all the cakes? Does it matter where you begin?

### Number Trains

Have students practise the number sequence when lined up (e.g. to enter or leave the classroom). Ask each student to count in turn from one to determine 'how many' students are in the line. Ask: Could we find out how many are here if we count by 2s? Will we get the same number?

### Biggest Number

Ask students to choose and use materials to show why seven is less than eight when counting a collection. Focus on the idea that the next number names a quantity which must always be one more than the number before.

### Grouping

Invite students to rearrange a collection of things to make them easier to count (e.g. counting to see how many students are at school today). Ask: Can we arrange ourselves so it is easy to count? Is there another way? Record the totals each time, then ask: What do you notice about how many we get every time we count? Why don't we get a different number if we start with a different person?

### Choosing Equipment

Ask students to set out equipment for an activity (e.g. art activity) by referring to the number of students and collecting enough equipment for each. To begin, place one chair for each student at a table, then stand a sign on the table saying what equipment is needed (e.g. paintbrush, scissors).

Each person needs a brush and a pair of scissors

### Different Totals

When the class is counting a collection and some students arrive at different totals for the same amount, have students consider whether or not this is possible. Ask: Could we all be right? Why? Why not?

# Beginning ✔✔✔

### Everyday Counting

Use real counting opportunities (e.g. deciding how many students are going swimming, or how much material is needed for an activity) to show students how counting is used by people in everyday situations.

### Matching

Organise the class into different-sized groups of students. Select a student in each group to collect and hand out enough sheets of paper to all members of their group. When each student collects the paper for their group, ask: Have you got the right amount of paper for your group? Will you have to come back for more paper, or will you return some sheets to me? How could you check? Focus on students' answers that include one-for-one matching and counting. Ask: Will counting help? (See Sample Lesson 2, page 22.)

### Enough for All

Invite students to suggest ways that they can check if there will be enough equipment for different numbers of people in different situations. For example, for small groups, ask a student to collect enough plastic cups for everyone at the table. For large groups, have students plan to collect enough beanbags for an activity to be held the following day. Give a reason for bringing just enough beanbags for the group; for example, say: Another class wants the left-over beanbags, so we can't take the whole box. How will we know when we have enough beanbags for our group? How could you check to see if there will be enough beanbags?

### Placing an Order

Have students use plastic (play dough) food for a role play. One student could be a delivery person to whom the other students phone through an order. Encourage students to think about whether they will have enough of each thing for their group. Ask: How will the delivery person know if there is enough food for everyone? Focus students on ways to decide what is enough. When students count to find out how many they need, ask: How will counting help the delivery person bring enough food?

### Constant Addition

Ask students to use the constant function on a calculator to count groups of things. For example, to count how many legs on five chairs, students key in `1` `+` `=` for the first leg, then `=` for each remaining leg. Have students record how many legs. Repeat the count by 4s for each set of legs; for example, press `4` `+` `=` for the first chair, then `=` `=` `=` for each successive chair. Record how many legs. Ask: Should we get the same result each time? Why? Why not?

## Skip Counting a Large Collection

Have students select a number to use when skip counting a large collection. Ask: Why did you choose that number? Why wouldn't you choose to skip count by 7s or 8s? Then, extend the activity by asking students to choose a different number to re-count. Ask: Did you get the same result? Why? Why not?

## Skip Counting Money

Have students skip count by five cents, ten cents, and so on, up to and over $1. Then, extend the activity by asking students to skip count by $1, $5 and $10, up to and over $100.

### *Did You Know?*

Students can use their calculators to record a count. For example, students could count the number of bikes in the school's bike racks to find out how many students ride to school. To begin, students key in **1** **+** and then press **=** as they point the calculator at each item (i.e. **1** **+** **=** **=** **=** ). The calculator will display 1, 2, 3, and so on, as students repeatedly press the equal key. There is no need for students to press **+** **1** each time.

Similarly, 2 followed by **+** **=** **=** **=** **=** , and so on, counts by 2s. The first press of the equals key displays 2 and successively pressing the equals key signs displays 4, 6, 8, and so on. This is called constant addition.

It is also possible to do constant multiplication.

# SAMPLE LEARNING ACTIVITIES

## Middle ✔

### Large Collections

Have students collect a large quantity (e.g. 1000) of ring pulls, popsicle sticks, bread tags. Then, ask students to list the ways they could check how many. Ask: If we counted by 5s, then by 10s, would we get the same total? Would the total be the same if we counted by 4s?

### Which Number Is Bigger?

Ask students to say which of two numbers (e.g. 26 and 27) is bigger. Then, invite them to explain how they could convince someone that this has to be so.

### Counting On

Arrange some MAB materials or bundled materials so there are some ones, some tens, then some more ones, more tens, and so on. Invite students to count on by 1s and 10s to say how many little blocks altogether. Cover the blocks with a piece of card and gradually uncover the materials as the count proceeds.

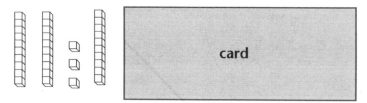

Ask: Does the total change if we start the count from the right instead of the left? Extend the activity to include hundreds blocks.

### Constant Addition

Ask students to use the constant function on their calculators to help count money. Use `10` `+` `=` `=` `=` to count 10-cent coins, then change to `+` `20` `=` `=` to count 20-cent coins, and `+` `50` `=` `=` to count 50-cent coins. Ask: How much money do we have? Would this be the same if we started with the 50-cent coins?

### Running Totals

Ask students to maintain a progressive count of objects that they have collected throughout the year (e.g. popsicle sticks, craft sticks) to make Christmas gifts. Have students deposit their objects in a box. Ask them to count the objects each day and then empty them into a larger box. Record a daily running total. Ask: How do you know that the total in the box must be the same as the new total we write down each day?

**Bucket Loads**

Have students focus on counting requirements when estimating the size of very large collections (e.g. grains of sand, beans, peas, matches). Ask: How many grains of sand (beans, peas, matches) in a bucket? Invite students to count how many grains of sand (beans, peas, matches) in a teaspoonful, then how many teaspoonfuls in a tablespoon, then how many tablespoons in a cup, and how many cups in a bucket. Ask: What changed in each successive count? Can you use the constant function on your calculators to progressively count out the increasing equal quantities of grains? What would you expect to find if you actually counted every grain of sand (bean, pea, match) one by one?

## SAMPLE LESSON 1

**Sample Learning Activity:** Beginning—'Teeth', page 14

**Key Understanding 1:** We can count a collection to find out how many are in it.

**Focus:** Counting each item exactly once

**Working Towards:** Level 1

### Students' Purpose for Counting

As part of a Society and Environment topic, the students in Kerri's class created portraits of themselves for a classroom display. After looking at the portraits, the students decided they would like to know how many in their class had a front tooth missing. Some of the students were worried because they hadn't drawn their teeth, so the class decided to count the real people.

### Challenging Existing Ideas

The students sorted themselves into three groups—students without gaps in their teeth, students with gaps, and those without gaps but with half-grown teeth in some places. While the students were counting how many in their group, a debate began in one of the groups. Jane's count was 12; Inger's count was 14. The difference in the count resulted in a whole-class discussion about whether it was all right to get different answers.

'You could if you missed someone out,' said Bo-lu.

'Someone might have moved,' said another.

'There's lots to count in that group,' was another response.

*Not all students of this age will be bothered by Jane and Inger getting a different count. The discussion might go right over the heads of such students.*

## Drawing Out the Mathematical Ideas

Kerri saw the opportunity to focus on the need to count every item once and once only, so she asked the students to watch Jane and Inger re-count for the group. 'I wonder what they will do to make sure they are counting everyone in the whole group,' Kerri said to the class.

Inger asked each person to sit down as she counted them and arrived at a total of 12.

Jane touched each person on the head, but then forgot where she had started. 'I think I'll have to put them in a line,' she said. 'Then, I'll know if I've counted everyone.'

The students were delighted when Inger's count was the same as Jane's. 'So, now we really know how many kids have front teeth missing.'

Next, the students moved on to sorting their portraits on the basis of age. This came about as a result of someone suggesting that big front teeth grow when you are six years old. The five-year-old group arranged their portraits in a line, so 'we don't miss any like we did with our teeth,' and the other group followed suit. Kerri was satisfied with what they had achieved.

> *Inger and Jane know that they need to 'touch' each person exactly once as they say the number names in order. Do they understand why?*

## Feedback on What Students Really Understand

However, Kerri's confidence was shaken just a few minutes later:

*The class recorded how many students were in the five-year-old group and in the six-year-old group. They talked about the strategy they had learnt for counting. Then, I asked them to count their group again. This time, I asked the students to begin the count at the other end of the line of drawings. Many students predicted there would be a different total and were quite surprised at the result. As if to drive the point home, one of the doubters said with complete confidence, 'But I think it really will be different if we start in the middle.'*

Kerri plans to provide many more opportunities for counting where the students are challenged to think about whether it makes sense to get a different number if you count the collection in different ways. Her major purpose for the near future will be to ensure that she draws this important mathematical idea out of the counting activities she provides for her students.

> *Understanding that it does not make sense to get different counts for the same collection is necessary for the achievement of Level 2.*

## SAMPLE LESSON 2

**Sample Learning Activity:** Beginning—'Matching', page 16

**Key Understanding 1:** We can count a collection to find out how many are in it.

**Focus:** Deciding to count to make matching sets

**Working Towards:** Levels 1 and 2

### Connecting Counting to Everyday Experience

*Students may know how to count quite well, but they may not use this strategy to make matching sets, such as collecting a straw for each student.*

Ruth knew her Year 1 students could count quite well. She also made a point of providing them with opportunities to count for real purposes. For example, Ruth would ask the students to get enough brushes (sheets of paper, cups) from the art trolley for their group. These tasks are real and the situations provide direct feedback.

Ruth noticed, however, that many students did not choose to count unless she specifically suggested counting or used the words 'how many' to cue them to count. Then, Ruth realised that the students usually worked in small groups, so they were able to remember all the group members and collect 'one each' by name. Other students would simply collect several and return any spares or go back for more. While Ruth had provided the students with situations where they could count, they could do it another way and so did not need to count.

### Challenging Existing Ideas

*Seeing other students use counting as a strategy for collecting the right number of brushes may challenge a student to try it.*

Ruth thought that reorganising the students into larger groups might challenge them to count. One day, she separated the students into three different-sized groups. She casually asked three students to collect enough paper to give everyone in their group a sheet. Ruth did not tell the students to count or to work out 'how many'. Her focus was on whether the students would choose to count in a practical situation and whether they trusted the count enough to rely on it.

As the students returned to their groups, Ruth called the class to attention and asked the three students if they had the correct number of sheets. 'Do you have to return any sheets or do you have to go back for more?' Ruth asked.

Leah said that she had taken a pile of paper she thought would be about right. Danni was confident hers would be exactly right. Craig shrugged. He thought it would be all right.

Ruth asked Leah how she could check. Leah suggested handing out the sheets to her group. Then, Ruth asked the other two what they thought. They agreed with Leah's suggestion. Ruth said, 'Yes, seems sensible to me.' Ruth then indicated that the three students should hand out their sheets of paper. Leah discovered she was short and had to go back for more paper.

After a pause, Ruth commented, 'Popping back to get more paper isn't a problem when the paper is in the classroom, but suppose you had to walk all the way to the Resource Centre. It would be better if you could get the exact amount, wouldn't it?' She continued, 'How could you have made sure?'

The students suggested several strategies, including making a list of the students in their group and trying to remember who was in their group. Danni said she counted the number of students in her group.

Then, Ruth asked the students to think about which strategy they liked the best. Ruth suggested that counting was quicker than writing a list. She also suggested that it was easier to remember a number than all the students' names. Once counting was suggested, the students tended to agree that it was a good idea. When Ruth asked if counting would always give the right amount, a vocal group insisted it would.

However, Ruth was under no illusion that all the students always trust the count to work, or that most would choose to count next time. Ruth repeated this kind of activity regularly as the students went about other classroom activities, making sure not to cue them that she wanted them to count.

> *Teaching activities for children [in this phase] clearly need to involve the children in a variety of situations where counting is a good strategy for solving problems and where they can make inferences on the basis of counting. Their use of this general strategy in meaningful situations is expected to make Number more meaningful to them. In other words, teaching at this age level may have the aim of making counting a thinking tool.*
>
> **Nunes and Bryant, p. 43**

## KEY UNDERSTANDING 2

*We can often see how many are in a collection just by looking and also by thinking of it in parts.*

Most very young students can recognise collections of one, two or three things without counting, simply by looking at the collection as a whole. This 'seeing how many at a glance' is often called 'subitising'. It develops before counting and underpins it.

Later, students 'see' that two looks different from and less than three and come to connect this with the counting sequence. Students who do not readily distinguish 'oneness', 'twoness' and 'threeness' just by looking are unlikely to benefit from counting experiences. They need explicit help to develop the capacity to subitise small numbers. Students who can subitise one, two and three should be assisted to extend this to collections of five, six and beyond. Using environmental stimuli, such as small handfuls of beans exposed briefly by opening and closing the palm, or birds flying overhead, as well as flashcards are relevant strategies to assist this development.

Some young students who are not able to say the number names in order, nevertheless have learned to recognise six or seven real objects 'at a glance' through family games and activities. The significance of this capability should not be overlooked since such students are likely to be disadvantaged if it is assumed that there is only one order in which they can learn about numbers. The skill of seeing how many at a glance could form the basis for further number work, much as counting does for other students.

Students should also learn to think of a collection in component parts, coming to see that:

• it is easier to see how many there are when collections are in special arrangements:

●●●
●●●
●●●

and, in later years, perhaps with MAB blocks:

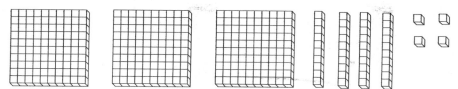

* any collection can be separated into parts and each part can be represented by a number; thinking 'part-part-whole' can help us to see 'how many' there are. For example, in this array, some students might say, *I see 3, 5, which is 8.* (Another student might see 3, 4, 1 or 3, 3, 2.)

* the same number can be thought of in parts in different ways:

   6     1         5     2        3     4        7

* a number can also be thought of in more than two parts:

  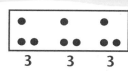

     9          3   3   3

Counting is important but too much emphasis on one-to-one counting as the only way to decide 'how many' can make students overly reliant on immature counting-based strategies. This may actually delay students' development of a sense of the size of numbers and their flexibility in dealing with them. The knowledge that you can 'break up' a quantity and move bits from one group to another without changing the overall quantity must be linked in students' minds to what they know about numbers from counting. This enables students to come to trust a number as signifying a quantity that does not change as a result of counting differently, or rearranging parts, or rewriting in a different form.

While students need many counting experiences, as described in Key Understanding 1, teaching should emphasise equally decomposing or partitioning collections into parts. Activities should help students to see that any number can be thought of as a sum or difference of other numbers in several different ways.

KU **2**

This:

- provides a basis for understanding what addition and subtraction mean (Understand Operations)

- helps students to see why, when two collections are combined, counting on from one of the numbers must give the same result as counting the whole collection from the start (Calculate)

- enables students to count large collections efficiently by counting in groups (skip counting) and also to understand why the technique must give the same result as counting in ones.

Each of these is integral to achievement of Level 2 of the outcome. Partitioning activities also provide a foundation for progress towards Level 3. This is because the capacity to think flexibly of numbers as the sum and the difference of other numbers underpins the understanding of place value and all effective mental and written computation. (See also Calculate, especially Key Understanding 2.)

## SAMPLE LEARNING ACTIVITIES

### Beginning ✔✔✔

#### Collecting

Have students pick up a collection of two blocks, then three blocks, from a group of blocks without counting. Increase the number to five if students are successful at each amount.

#### Separating Collections

Invite pairs of students to investigate how a collection can be separated into parts. For example, students take turns to drop a collection of beans and tell their partner the size of the groups the collection is separated into (e.g. a collection of eight beans may fall into groups of 4 and 3 and 1.) Students then record these groupings both pictorially and numerically. Compile each pair's results into a class chart to use in future lessons.

#### Dice Combinations

Organise students into pairs. Give each pair two dice. Have students take turns to roll the dice and then say how many dots just by looking. Ask: How many dots are on the first die? (e.g. 2) How many dots on the second die? (e.g. 3) How many dots altogether? (e.g. 5) Have students use calculators to keep progressive scores. The first student to a given number (e.g. 50) could be the winner. Later, extend the activity to include three dice.

### How Many?

Flash small groups of things (e.g. leaves, stones) to students. Ask them to say how many at a glance without one-to-one counting.

### Flashcards

Show students a flashcard with, for example, seven things in groupings of 5 and 2. Ask: How many things are there? What helped you see how many are there? (Link to Calculate, Key Understanding 1.)

### Snap

Organise students into pairs. Have students use adhesive dots or drawings to make sets of cards with groupings of up to six spots randomly placed. When playing, have students say the number of spots on the cards if there is a match. Later, add number cards where students match numbers to spots arranged in domino patterns up to 10. (Link to Calculate, Key Understanding 2.)

### Straws

Have each student hide five straws under the desk, some in each hand. Then, invite all students to show one hand. Ask those students with the same number of straws revealed to stand up and compare their groupings. Ask: Do you all have the same number of straws in the other hand? Have students record their groupings for five straws, then try different arrangements. Focus on the part-whole relationships of the numbers. Repeat the activity and gradually include more straws. (Link to Calculate, Key Understanding 2.)

### Five Little Monkeys

Use story contexts to help students group numbers in an organised way. For example, give students five monkey templates (e.g. photos cut from magazines) to move from tree to tree. Begin with one monkey in a small tree and four in a large tree. Say: There are four monkeys in the first tree and one monkey in the second tree. Move one monkey so that there are three monkeys in one tree and two monkeys in the other. Then, ask: Are there still five monkeys altogether? Repeat the activity for combinations of 2 and 3, 1 and 4, and 0 and 5.

### Hands Up

Have two students face each other, then clap their hands three times before holding up between five and ten fingers. Have them show all the fingers on one hand and some extra fingers on the second hand. Together, students say how many fingers are held up altogether. (Link to Calculate, Key Understandings 1 and 4.)

## SAMPLE LEARNING ACTIVITIES

### Middle ✔✔

**Number Scatters**

Have students glance at a scatter of between five and 20 sticky dots on a flashcard and say how many dots are on the card. Rotate the card so that students see different groupings from different directions. Ask: What groups of dots did you see from where you are sitting? Repeat the activity with different cards showing a range of different arrangements.

**Investigating Collections**

Invite students to investigate multiple collections of things in the environment (e.g. egg cartons, muffin trays, packets of stock cubes). Have students record the arrangements that help them to see how many there are. (Link to Calculate, Key Understandings 2 and 3.)

**Ten Frames**

Flash counters on a ten frame on an overhead projector and ask students to write a number sentence for the groups that they see. Answers might include: *I see 5 + 2. I see 3 + 2 + 2.*

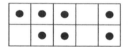

Ask students to explain how they saw the groups (See Middle Sample Learning Activities in Calculate, Key Understanding 2.)

**Combining Groups**

Use two ten frames to extend the above activity. Fill one ten frame and part fill the other. Then, ask students to say how many by 'seeing' the group of 10 and then some more for all of the 'teen' numbers. Later, ask students to 'see' two different groups (e.g. 8 + 4), and combine them to say how many.

 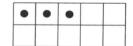

**Snap**

Refer to the rules of this game in the Beginning Sample Learning Activities (page 27). Use groupings up to 18. Have students use increasingly larger numbers as they become more confident.

**Playing Cards**

Flash overhead transparencies that show playing cards (excluding face cards). Invite students to say what groups they see; for example, looking at the 8 of hearts card, one student might see: 3 + 3 + 2; another might see 2 + 2 + 2 + 2. Rotate the card so that it is in a different direction and ask students to look for different groups, for example:

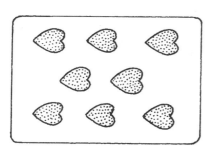 

Later, cut the numbers off the card. Ask students to use their groups to say how many shapes on the card.

**How Many Altogether**

Extend the 'Playing Cards' activity by using two cards together and asking students to use the groupings to say how many altogether.

**Arrays**

Show students rectangular arrays (e.g. 3 x 4) of dots, squares or pictures of everyday objects (e.g. cups) on card or overhead projector. Ask: How many equal groups do you see? How many in each group? How many altogether? Rotate the card and repeat. Ask: Do you see different groups? (See Calculate, Key Understanding 3.)

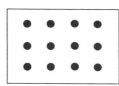 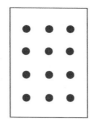

# SAMPLE LEARNING ACTIVITIES

## Later ✔✔

### Large Collections

Briefly show students large scattered collections of things. For example, flash at least 110 dots on an overhead projector; pause at a scene on a video that shows, say, a large herd of animals at a waterhole; or spill a container of beans. Ask: How many are there? How did you work it out? Are there any other ways that would help us to know 'how many' without counting?

### Squares and Triangles

Have students investigate numbers to see which collections can be arranged as a square or a triangle. Ask students to draw and display the arrangements as square and triangular numbers, then give each arrangement a label (e.g. 9 is $3^2$). Later, have students play 'Snap'. Ask them to match an 'arrangement' card to a number card in order to practise recognition of how many in each collection.

## Working Out Quantities

Invite pairs of students to work out quantities by looking at groups of materials (e.g. straws or matchsticks). Have each pair take a quantity of blocks. One partner groups or partitions the blocks while the other quickly looks and says how many there are (e.g. *I knew there were 32 blocks because I saw four in each group, and I know 8 x 4 = 32*). Extend the activity to focus on large numbers using MAB materials and fractional numbers using pattern blocks. (See Calculate, Key Understandings 2 and 3.)

## Place-Value Partitioning

Have students use place-value partitioning to see at a glance how many are in a collection. Use the overhead projector to quickly show arrays of 1, 10, 100, 1000 and 10 000 cut out from 1 millimetre grid paper and ask: How did you know it was 1000? Then, say: Sketch the array that is ten lots of 100 (10 000). Write the numbers for each. Ask: How many squares are on the 1 millimetre page? How did you work it out?

## Grid Partitions

Invite pairs of students to practise recognising partitions of 100. For example, students use 2 mm squared paper and draw a line to partition a 100 square into two parts.

34 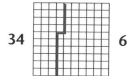 66

Ask: Where would you draw the line so that your partner can say how many in each part at a glance? Then, using a new 100 square each time, students take it in turns to see how quickly they can recognise the two parts of 100. Ask students to share strategies that make this recognition easy. Repeat the activity, but have students imagine that the 100 square is equal to $1. (See Calculate, Key Understanding 2.)

## Thousand Grid

Extend the above activity using a 1000 grid. Invite students to say how they can see at a glance how many hundreds, tens and ones in each of the two parts. Discuss how their strategies differ from those used in the 'Grid Partitions' activity.

423        577

## KEY UNDERSTANDING 3

*We can use numbers in ways that do not refer to quantity.*

When we count a collection or measure something we are using numbers to describe quantity. However, numbers are also used in other ways, which do not imply quantity. Number names can be used to describe the relative position or place of things in a sequence, that is, the order in which things occur. We expect page 16 to be between pages 15 and 17. We are irritated if room 4 is not directly between rooms 3 and 5. In the library, a book with Dewey number 3.15 should be found between books numbered 3.141 and 3.2. We say first, second and third when we understand that the third page in the sequence is the same as page 3.

Students should understand that when we use numbers to describe the order in which things occur, we are not describing quantity. For example, in a competition we do not expect the difference between first and second place to be the same as the difference between second and third place. We also do not expect the same number of books (or shelf distance) to lie between Dewey numbers 3.15 and 3.16 as between Dewey numbers 4.71 and 4.72. We also do not expect a book with Dewey number of 4.16 to be twice as far along a shelf as a book with the number 2.08. This is why it does not usually make sense to add, subtract or average numbers when they are used only to describe order.

While it does not make sense to think of ordinal numbers as quantities, we do use place value when using numbers to order. For example, we know that the 940th page in the telephone book will occur after any of the pages in the 800s just by looking at the hundreds place.

Students who have achieved Level 1 of the outcome will use small numbers to describe the position of things they can see and remember, and to select a particular person, object or event. They use words such as first, second and third appropriately in familiar and practical situations. These students would be amused to hear their younger siblings saying, as some do, 'I came first second.' They now know what 'first' and 'second' mean.

Students who have achieved Level 2 can also order using numbers with which they have no immediate concrete experience. They know, for example, that if they finished 216th in a marathon, they came in after a person who was 210th. These students also distinguish counting a collection, where the count signifies quantity, from using numbers to signify order.

Sometimes, numbers are used in ways that do not signify an inherent order or quantity. Rather, they are used to label things in the same way that we use the letters of the alphabet. We may then use the order of the numbers to make sorting and finding the things easier—again, as we do letters—but the numbers do not describe an inherent order or quantity. For instance, a suburb with postcode 6056 need not be between suburbs with postcodes 6055 and 6057, and the latter suburb is not necessarily bigger than the former.

Similarly, when numbers are used to label categories, such as types of cars or teams, no order or quantity is implied. It makes no sense to add, subtract or average these sorts of numbers. Also, 'label' numbers do not have place value (i.e. the postcode 6055 is read as 'six-zero-five-five'), and spacing of the numbers does not necessarily occur in groups of three. These ideas link more closely with the outcomes for Contextualising Mathematics in the Working Mathematically strand.

**KU 3**

# SAMPLE LEARNING ACTIVITIES

## Beginning ✔✔

### Ordinal Numbers

Have four students stand in a line in front of the class. Decide with the class which student is first, second, third and fourth. Then, ask students to close their eyes while the line is reshuffled. Ask: Who is first now? Who is in the third place? Is this place always second?

### Hungry Caterpillar

Read *The Very Hungry Caterpillar* by Eric Carle with the class. Invite students to recall the order of the events in the story. Ask questions, such as: What did the caterpillar eat on the third day (Wednesday)? (See Reason About Number Patterns, Key Understanding 3. Link to Operations, Key Understanding 1.)

### Everyday Events

Ask students to make an ordered list of jobs they need to complete before school (e.g. *First, I get out of bed. Second, I have breakfast* ...) Ask: What do you do fifth in the morning?

**Order in the Classroom**

Brainstorm classroom routines where students would benefit from establishing and using an order; for example, setting up a classroom computer roster. Have students list the users in order and number each one. Ask: What position are you? How many students get to use the computer before you?

**Patterns**

In groups, have students discuss the order of things (e.g. different-coloured blocks, tiles, beads) used in a pattern sequence they have made. Help students ask each other questions, such as: What will your tenth (twentieth) piece look like? Then, invite students to continue their patterns to find out, then record, which positions have the same coloured block (e.g. *My second, fourth, sixth, eighth and tenth blocks are all yellow triangles*). (Link to Reason About Number Patterns, Key Understanding 2.)

**Sports Stars**

Show a photograph of a sporting team to students. Invite each student to say the number on their favourite sporting star's uniform. Ask: Is the person with the number 1 jumper more important than the person with number 16?

**Phone Numbers**

Ask each student to write, then hold up their telephone number for others to read. Ask: Does anyone have the same phone number as you? Do they have part of your phone number? Which part? What does that part mean?

**Number Hunt**

During a walk around the school or neighbourhood, encourage students to find out where numbers are used and what they are used for. Pay particular attention to room, house and bus numbers, as well as car numberplates. Have students decide whether the numbers describe order. Ask: What do these numbers tell us about these rooms (houses, cars, buses)?

KU 3

## SAMPLE LEARNING ACTIVITIES

# Middle ✔

### Ordinal Numbers

Ask students to solve problems that involve ordinal numbers. For example, say: The second person in line has two people behind her. How many are in the line? There were nine bikes in a race. Six bikes were in front of Jack's bike at the finish line. In which position did Jack's bike finish? Then, ask students to pose some of their own ordinal number problems to the class or a partner.

### Dates

Have students read a series of dates out loud using ordinal numbers. Invite them to explain, for example, what the 'fourth' and 'sixth' refer to in 4/6/2004. Draw out the idea that while the numerals 4 and 6 refer to order, the 2004 refers to the number (quantity) of years.

### Newspaper Numbers

Ask students to circle all the numbers on the page of a newspaper, then write next to each number what it is for; for example, how many, which position, which one.

### Telephone Tactics

Have students make a directory of class members' phone numbers and local services that are of interest to them (e.g. vet, local swimming pool). Invite students to suggest ways of breaking up a number so that it can be easily said and remembered. Ask: Do these numbers show you how much of anything (quantity)? Is there any order in phone numbers? Why aren't they listed in the phone book in the order of the numbers?

### Buses

Invite students to use bus information, such as timetables, to record bus numbers and their destinations. Students then decide if there is a relationship between the number and the destination. Ask: Why do we have numbers on buses? Do they show how much of something?

### Postcode Particulars

Ask students to name towns across Australia and record their postcodes using postcode booklets or phone books. Discuss how different numbers (postcodes) are used in different States. Ask: Is it possible to draw a line on a map to show a connection between all of the postcodes across a State? Why do we use postcodes? As an extension activity, have students investigate how postcodes are used in other countries.

### Numberplates

Have students work in pairs to record the numberplates of cars passing the school. Then, ask each pair to sort the numbers and give reasons for these groupings. Later, have students examine the reasons why we use numberplates. Ask: Do numberplates show us how much of anything (quantity)? Do they show the order of anything? Although numberplates may have some letters or numbers in common, each numberplate is a label that distinguishes one car from every other vehicle. Personalised numberplates, such as 'MUM 167', are labels, but they also indicate that the person with this numberplate was the 167th person to choose that plate. Draw out the idea that although numberplates might be given out and filed in order, they are only used as labels like names.

KU 3

# SAMPLE LEARNING ACTIVITIES

## Later ✔

### Ordering Decimal Numbers

Ask students to use decimal numbers to put things in order in a range of practical situations. For example, ask students to keep the class's non-fiction library books in order using the Dewey system. Ask: What does the number 6.124 on the spine mean? Could this number represent the size of the book? Why? Why not? Does this number show how far apart the books are? What does it show?

### Order of Position

Have students collect and organise examples of how numbers indicate order in everyday situations. Make sure students differentiate between numbers that show order of position (e.g. tickets that show a seating number, or a first-place ribbon for athletics) and numbers that show order in time (e.g. the numbers on a pack of cake mix—which indicate what you do first, second, and so on).

### Numbers as Labels

Ask students to investigate how numbers are used as labels (e.g. postcode numbers). Then, have students invent a new suburb and place it between their town and a neighbouring town. Help students find postcodes for their new suburbs and see how their numbers relate to the adjacent suburbs. Ask: How would you work out what the postcode for your new suburb could be? (See also Middle Sample Learning Activities.)

### Numbers on Vehicles

Repeat the 'Numbers as Labels' activity with numberplates. Ask students to investigate the different categories of numberplates that are issued (e.g. taxis, trucks). Ask: How do we recognise these different categories? (See also Middle Sample Learning Activities.)

### Numbers and Food

Invite students to find out about the use of numbers as labels on food products. Students could collect barcodes and product numbers. Have students investigate what the numbers mean on different products. Ask: How can you find out what the food additives consist of from the numbers given?

### Did You Know?

In many libraries, people are asked not to put books back onto the shelves. It seems that many of us put a book coded 360.3417 after 360.56 on the shelf when it should come before. In other words, we treat a Dewey code as though it is two whole numbers separated by a decimal point.

This is not so surprising. Sometimes, a decimal point is used to separate two whole numbers. For example, in reports we often treat each side of the point separately so that the sections might be: 1.1, 1.2, … 1.9, 1.10, 1.11, … 2.1, 2.2, and so on.

When people place library books on the shelves incorrectly, it could be for two different reasons.

**Mathematical:** Some people may not understand how decimals work and actually think that the decimal point separates two whole numbers. This is a very common misconception.

**Contextual:** People may understand decimals, but they may not know that Dewey numbers are Dewey decimal numbers. They may think that Dewey numbers work like sections in a report.

Both forms of knowledge—the mathematical and contextual—are needed for numeracy and should be dealt with together in classrooms.

KU 3

## KEY UNDERSTANDING 4

*The whole numbers are in a particular order and there are patterns in the way we say them which help us to remember the order.*

One of the everyday meanings of 'to count' is to recite the whole number names in their right order. Realising that the numbers have a particular order and remembering the order are two of the learning challenges for young students, and this largely occurs orally. We need to assist students from an early age to notice the patterns in the way we say numbers; for example: *twenty*, twenty-one, ... twenty-nine, *thirty*, thirty-one, … ninety-nine, *one hundred*, one hundred and one, and so on. Students will need to use these patterns to say, for example, what comes after 79 and also what comes before 80, counting both forwards and backwards from any number.

Students need to understand that they do not have to remember every number name because the patterns in the numeration system enable us to predict a number even if we have never heard it before. In order to develop the capacity to generate any numbers in sequence, students need to:

- memorise the 1 to 13 words in sequence, since there is no inherent pattern in the sounds

- hear the 4 to 9 part of the sequence in 14 to 19 (although, 'fifteen' does not sound quite like 'fiveteen')

- predict and name the decades by following the 1 to 9 sequence

- repeat the 1 to 9 sequence within each decade

- predict and name the hundreds by following the 1 to 9 sequence

- repeat the decade sequence and 1 to 9 sequence within each of the hundreds

- predict and name the thousands by following the 1 to 9 sequence

- repeat the hundreds, decades and 1 to 9 sequences within each of the thousands

- except for the teens, say the places in the order in which the digits are written from left to right.

Our place-value system is based on powers of ten, so that 2567 means '2 tententens + 5 tentens + 6 tens + 7 ones'. We know 'tentens' is called a hundred, so '5 tentens' can be said 'five hundred'. Also, we know 'tententens' is ten hundreds, which is called a thousand, so '2 tententens' is said 'two thousand'. Having come this far, some students will generalise the pattern further and predict that ten thousands will be millions. This is a reasonable prediction, given the pattern so far, but it is not the way our numeration system works. In order to be able to read and say numbers beyond the thousands, students will need considerable experience of the cyclical role of each set of three places. Thus, we have the first set of three places: ones, tens and hundreds; followed by the second set of three places: the ones of thousands, tens of thousands and hundreds of thousands, and so on. The way we *say* large numbers is based on powers of a thousand, with the pattern in the initial ones, tens and hundreds being repeated.

**KU 4**

| one | hundreds | tens | ones | hundreds | tens | ones | hundreds | tens | ones |
|-----|----------|------|------|----------|------|------|----------|------|------|
| billions | millions | | | thousands | | | ones | | |
| 4 | 0 | 2 | 7 | 3 | 4 | 6 | 4 | 2 | 7 |

The spaces in 4 027 346 427 signal this cyclical process in speech. This allows us to say bigger and bigger numbers and to get a feel for their order of magnitude.

However, it is important to note, that the thousands cycle applies only to whole numbers. We do not use it in the decimal places, saying the digits *after* the decimal point one at a time. For example, 267.267 is said 'two hundred and sixty-seven point two six seven'. Also, 206 is said 'two hundred and six', skipping the zero, but .206 is 'point two zero six'. The distinction between how we say the numbers on either side of the decimal point should be made explicit, since saying a number such as 45.67 as 'forty-five point sixty-seven' may perpetuate the misconception that the decimal point simply separates two whole numbers.

Students who have achieved Level 1 can say the number names in order into the teens. Those students at Level 2 can use the decades up to and over 100 and count backwards and forwards from numbers to a hundred.

At Level 3, students will readily use the names of the first several places from the right (ones, tens, hundreds, thousands), but may find larger whole numbers difficult to read and say.

Students who have achieved Level 4 understand and use the cyclical pattern in whole numbers and so can read the number in the diagram on the previous page as 'Four *billion*, twenty-seven *million*, three hundred and forty-six *thousand*, four hundred and twenty-seven'. At Level 5, students can say and read any decimal number.

## SAMPLE LEARNING ACTIVITIES

### Beginning ✔✔✔

#### Jack-in-the-Box

Have students play games that involve chanting numbers. Initially, ask students to count into the teens. Then, have students choose a number between 10 and 20. In unison, the class counts up to the chosen number and one student, playing the role of 'Jack', jumps up in the air. Similarly, have students count down from a selected number to one, then the class calls out 'Blast off!'

#### Numbers and Objects

Display collections of 13 to 19 objects that are found in the classroom (e.g. pencils) and their matching number. Arrange the objects in ways that highlight the way the number is said; for example, 14 pencils can be arranged as:

#### Numbers and Actions

Ask students to count aloud matching the count to the rhythm of actions; for example, skips with a rope, hops with a hoop, or catches of a ball.

#### Number Line

Invite students to make a number line around the room in chunks of numbers (e.g. 0 to 10). Begin with the range 0 to 10, then add 11, 12, 13 to 19, 20, 21 to 29, and so on. Ask: What sounds the same about the new numbers? How does each new number sound different from the others? Before counting from 1, focus students' attention on when the number pattern sounds different (e.g. from 12 to 13, from 19 to 20). Ask: What comes after 13 (14, 15)? What parts of the twenties sounds the same as the thirties?

## Number Scrolls

Ask students to generate number sequences using the constant function on their calculators over the decades and hundreds. Then, have students read, say, predict and verify the numbers from the calculator display. (Link to Reason About Number Patterns, Key Understandings 5; Calculate, Key Understanding 9.)

## Counting Sequences

Ask the class to form a line. Beginning at 1, have students say in turn the next number in the counting sequence, going down the line and then back again. Over time, begin the count at, say 8, 18, 25, 30, 48, 95 to extend the count into the larger numbers.

## Biggest Number

Select students to write the biggest number they know at the top of a display board. Ask each student: What is one more? Write the new number beneath the first. Then, have students add to the sequence each day and say the new number. Ask: Can this number sequence come to an end?

## Hundred Charts

Invite students to fill in their own 1 to 100 charts using the constant function on their calculators. They can start from any number between 1 and 9. Then, organise students into pairs. One student reads aloud the numbers in the chart vertically by tens while their partner keys in the agreed starting number (e.g. 3) and constantly adds **10** . Encourage the student with the chart to call stop at any time, then ask: What number will be next? Have students check the calculator display against the chart.

| 1 | 3 | 7 |
|---|---|---|
| 11 | 13 | 17 |
| 21 | 23 | 27 |
| 31 | 33 | 37 |
| 41 | 43 | 47 |
| 51 | 53 | 57 |
| 61 | 63 | 67 |
| 71 | 73 | 77 |
| 81 | 83 | 87 |
| 91 | 93 | 97 |

KU 4

## SAMPLE LEARNING ACTIVITIES

### Middle ✔✔ ~~grades 3-5~~

#### Next Number

Ask the class to say number names in order. For example, the first student begins with 81, then each student in turn says the next number up to and over 100. Extend the activity by having students begin the count at 201, or count from 560 to 630 (970 to 1110). Stop the class count at change-over points (e.g. 89, 209, 590) and ask: How do you know what number should be next? Further extend the activity by asking students to count backwards, or by 5s (10s).

#### Constant Numbers

Extend the range of numbers in the 'Next Number' activity using the constant function on a calculator.

#### Extending Patterns

Place a 1 to 100 chart (i.e. 10 x 10 grid) in the middle of the board for students to choose a column or a row to extend in one direction. For example, in the 3, 13, 23 column a student says what the pattern is and then extends this pattern outside of the chart. For example, the pattern is +10 or −10, so to continue upwards, −3, −13, −23, and so on. Ask: How far could each line extend?

#### Bicycle Odometer

Have students make a bicycle odometer. Ask students to write the numbers 0 to 9 vertically on four strips of paper. Then, have them cut four squares in the piece of card, wide enough to thread the strips of paper through. Thread each strip through a hole in the card. Form loops with the strips and join the ends with sticky tape. Ask students to decide what changes after each 9 in a sequence. Have them use the odometer to read a number sequence. Ask: What number is 1 more than 99 (109, 189, 1099)? Which numbers change when 1 is added to each 9? What is the pattern in these changes?

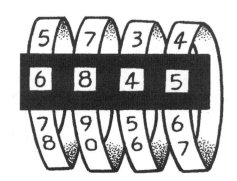

### Numbers as Words

Invite students to select a range of numbers, up to and including tens of thousands, and then write them as words. Select students to read their list of numbers out loud. Have other students listen for the word 'and'. Ask: Is 'and' used in the same way when we say 176 and 26 076?

### Comparing Numbers

Have students work in pairs. Ask one student to write down and then call out a 'really big number' for their partner to enter into the calculator. Have them compare the number on the screen with the written version of the number. Ask: Are they the same? If not, what do you think happened? How was the number said, or how was it heard? (Link to Calculate, Key Understanding 10.)

### Place Value

Ask students to enter **1**, then **0** into the calculator and say which place the 1 is in (*tens*). Have them add **0** and say where the 1 is now (*hundreds*). Continue recording the place names as they appear. Ask: How many places across does the 1 need to move in order to say 10 000 (1 000 000)? What is the pattern in the names of the places?

### Number Cards

Have students classify numbers by negotiating with each other to decide on the number groups. Give students a card with a number between 1000 and 10 000 000 and ask them to organise themselves into the appropriate groups. (e.g. *Our numbers are in the thousands.*) Ask: What does this group of numbers have in common? (See Sample Lesson 3, page 48.)

### Translating Numbers

Ask students to investigate literal translations of numbers from other cultures. For example, some Asian languages use 'ten, three' for thirteen; 'four tens, eight' for forty-eight. Then, have students organise materials (e.g. MAB blocks) to show each number and use this culture's way of counting.

KU 4

# SAMPLE LEARNING ACTIVITIES

## Later ✔✔

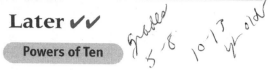

### Powers of Ten

Have students explore how place value helps us to add easily in powers of ten. For example, cover a mixed sequence of MAB blocks with a card. Then, uncover the blocks sequentially as students say the numbers.

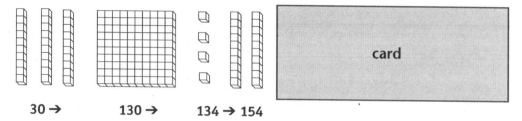

30 →       130 →       134 → 154

Ask: What patterns help you to say each new total so quickly?

### Continuing the Count

Have students use the patterns in the way we say numbers to continue the count up and over the tens and hundreds of thousands. Ask students to begin the count at crucial stages (e.g. 985, 9985, 99 985) and count forwards. Later, they can begin at a particular number (e.g. 9004, 10 004, 12 004) and count backwards.

### Predicting a Sequence

Invite pairs of students to predict a sequence of numbers. One student enters a seven-digit number into a calculator and reads the number out loud to their partner. Then, that student says the next twenty numbers, counting both forwards and backwards by 1s. The partner checks the count using the constant function.

### Counting Decimals

Ask students to say the counting sequence when using 0.1, 0.2, up to and over whole numbers (e.g. 3.7, 3.8, 3.9).

### Zero

Invite students to decide when zero is and is not said when saying a range of numbers. For example, have students sort a range of numbers—including 103, 9.05, 80, 800, 0.8, 270, 2703, 2.500—according to whether the zero is said or not. Make up a rule to share so it will be easy to decide next time. Ask: If your rule is 'whenever' there is a decimal point you say the zero, does it still apply to $1.05?

### Writing Large Numbers

Explore some common errors that are made when writing large numbers. Have students decide on the (erroneous) rule that could have produced the answer. For example, '100 004' instead of 'one million and four'; '20 000 364 123' instead of 'two million, three hundred and sixty-four thousand, one hundred and twenty-three'. Ask: What rule do you think is used for writing millions? Why doesn't that rule always work? (Link to Key Understanding 5)

### Car Odometer

Extend the Middle Sample Learning Activity ('Bicycle Odometer', page 44) to more places by adding more strips to the odometer.

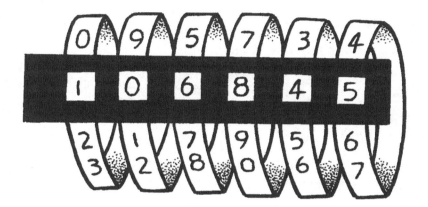

KU 4

### Measuring Heights

Have students work out what is different about the way we say the digits on either side of the decimal point. For example, ask students to use tape measures, then record their heights in metres and centimetres (e.g. 1 m 53 cm) and metres (e.g. 1.53 m). Discuss: What is different about how we say these numbers? Why doesn't it make sense to say 'one point fifty-three'? Plot students' heights on a graph for a classroom display. Revisit this graph later in the year, so students can gauge how much they have grown and practise saying decimal numbers.

### Solar System

Ask students to carry out investigations involving large numbers. For example, students could use the Internet to find the distance of satellites (the planets, the moon) from Earth. Ask: What did you have to do in order to say the distances out loud? Then, say: Rewrite the distances to help others to read the numbers aloud more easily. Do you always do this for long decimals? Why? Why not?

## SAMPLE LESSON 3

**Sample Learning Activity:** Middle—'Number Cards', page 45

**Key Understanding 4:** The whole numbers are in a particular order and there are patterns in the way we say them which helps us remember the order.

**Focus:** Reading numbers into the thousands and millions

**Working Towards:** Levels 3 and 4

*Many upper-primary students will tell you that a million is a thousand thousands, but they may still have difficulty actually reading and writing numbers beyond 9999. Often students have little sense of the relative magnitude of the numbers involved or place-value relationships beyond 1000.*

### Setting the Scene

Sally was surprised how difficult many of her Year 5 students found reading whole numbers that they had keyed into their calculators. Sally realised that the difficulty was with numbers that had more than four digits. The students were confident with the first three places and most extended this to the next place, which they called the thousands.

'Then, there's the millions,' said James. 'I know when it's one million, there are six zeros. See, like this. But, I think it must be when there are other numbers, not zeros, on the calculator that this is the millions.' James pointed to the fifth position. 'Yes, ones, tens, hundreds, thousands, millions.'

### Planning to Focus on the Mathematical Idea

Sally wanted to help her students see the repeated cyclical pattern of hundreds, tens and ones inherent in the place-value system.

*I decided on a classifying task. This meant students had to identify common characteristics of a range of large numbers. Each student was given a number card, with numbers ranging up to tens of millions. I decided not to have students generate the numbers on their calculators because the calculator display does not include a space between the groups of three digits, and I thought the spaces would help them in their search for the patterns. I also wanted to select numbers that would help the students' learning rather than leave this to chance.*

After handing out the number cards, Sally said, 'Look carefully at other people's numbers. Make a group with people who have a number that has something in common with yours.'

Eventually, the students realised they could fit into a number of groups. Apart from encouraging thoughtful groupings, Sally left the students to come up with their own classifications. Sally felt that her students' reasons for accepting or rejecting members into 'their' group told her a lot about their understanding.

One group had settled on a classification of 'thousands' when they saw that all of their numbers could also be classified as 'parts of a million'.

'I'm five hundred thousand. That's half a million,' said Marina.

Sally was pleased that this task also provided opportunities for students whose understanding of the repeated pattern of the number system was already quite advanced.

## Drawing Out the Important Ideas

When the students reported their classifications to the whole class, Sally recorded key words on the board. Classifications not linked to place value (e.g. 'We all have patterns in our numbers 25 25 25 and 187 187') weren't going to help Sally to draw out the cyclical repetition of the hundreds, tens and ones. Reference to the number of digits or reference to number names (e.g. millions) were the most useful.

Ben's group said, 'All of our numbers have six digits. One of the numbers is 120 000.'

Ashana's group said, 'All of our numbers—such as two thousand, four hundred and twenty-six—have four digits.'

## Challenging Existing Ideas

Sally used these reports to challenge students' thinking. 'So, in one group, we have numbers with four digits and we've said thousands. And, in another group, we have numbers with six digits and people also said thousands. How can this be?'

In the exchange of ideas that followed, Sally drew out from the students that 'the thousands' included 'ones of thousands' and 'tens of thousands', even 'hundreds of thousands'. However, it was only when the class decided to think about how the 'millions' looked, that the pattern of hundreds, tens and ones was clearly evident.

At this point, Sally drew their attention to the groupings of three digits, and the convention that spaces indicate the cycles of powers of a thousand. Sally wrote numbers between five and ten digits long on the board. Then, the students practised marking off the groups of three digits from the right to determine the starting point for reading the numbers.

KU 4

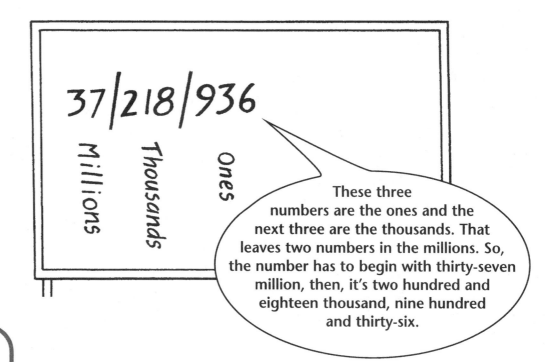

Those students who had a firm grasp of the idea could explain to other students that the pattern is the same even after they had run out of known names for groups. Sally said to the class, 'I wonder if there is a name for the group after billions.'

Some students pointed out that sometimes the spaces aren't put in. Eva said, 'What about on the calculator, when there are no spaces to show the groups of three digits?'

Sally drew out the idea that putting the spaces in, or imagining the spaces, can help us to get an idea of how big a number is (i.e. its magnitude) and of how to say it.

Sally plans to continue to investigate the thousands cycle with her class.

**THE METRIC SYSTEM**
*Before 1974, when Australia decimalised its measures, a comma was used to separate the powers of a thousand, and a full stop was inserted to separate the whole and fractional part of decimal numbers. However, the international system uses a space to separate the powers of a thousand and a comma in decimal numbers. Australia decided to stop using the comma in whole numbers for fifty years before starting to use it in decimals.*

### Did You Know?

Students may predict how the larger numbers are said and written. However, students get few opportunities to try out their predictions, so they don't get the feedback they need to refine their rules. Consider the following examples.

Some students think that each place has its own name and do not connect this with powers of ten. They may, for instance, think that the place immediately to the left of the thousands is the millions and read 56 706 as *5 million, 6 thousand, 7 hundred and 6*.

Other students think a new number name is used every time there is a new decade and so orally count *107, 108, 109, 200* and *1007, 1008, 1009, 2000*.

Sometimes, students write numbers as they hear them. They might write five hundred and six thousand, four hundred and thirty-one as *500 6000 431*.

It is important to ask students to write and say larger numbers in order to help them try out their personal rules and revise those that need it.

**KU 4**

# KEY UNDERSTANDING 5

*There are patterns in the way we write whole numbers that help us to remember their order.*

To read and write whole numbers, students need to be able to distinguish the 0 to 9 digits from other symbols, connect these symbols with their names, and learn how to put these symbols together to represent the whole numbers after 9. Key Understanding 7 deals with the extension of place value to include decimals. This Key Understanding is linked closely to Key Understanding 5 in Reason About Number Patterns.

Place value is the key to understanding how we say, read, write and calculate with whole numbers. It is the pattern in the way we put the digits together that enables us to write an infinite sequence of whole numbers and to easily put any two whole (or decimal) numbers in order.

Students have to understand the following important characteristics of our place-value system.

- The order of the digits makes a difference to the number, so 28 is different from 82.

- The position (or place) of a digit tells us the quantity it represents; for example, in 3526, the 2 indicates 2 tens or 20; but in 247, the 2 indicates 2 hundreds or 200.

- Zero is used as a place holder. It indicates there is none of a particular quantity and holds the other digits 'in place'; for example, 27 means 2 tens and 7 ones, but 207 means 2 hundreds, 0 tens and 7 ones.

- There is a constant multiplicative relationship between the places, with the values of the positions increasing in powers of ten, from right to left.

- To find the quantity that a digit represents, the value of the digit is multiplied by the value of the place; for example, in 3264, the 2 represents 200 because it is 2 x 100.

Students who have achieved Level 3 of the outcome have learned the names of the first several places from the right. They can also additively partition 2706 into 2 thousand + 7 hundred + 6. These students may not, however, really understand the multiplicative nature of the places—that is, the places show 2 x 1000, 7 x 100, 0 x 10, 6 x 1, respectively. This is an important feature of place value that helps us to read and write large and small numbers (see also Key Understandings 4 and 6), and to recognise their relative magnitude; for example, 6540 is ten times as much as 654 (which is central to Key Understanding 8).

Students who have achieved Level 4 fully understand and flexibly use whole-number place value—that is, they have brought together both its additive and multiplicative aspects. Students who have achieved Level 5 have generalised this to include decimal numbers and are fully operational in their use of the decimal notation system.

KU **5**

## SAMPLE LEARNING ACTIVITIES

### Beginning ✔✔

**Number Labels**

Ask students to write temporary number labels to show, for example, how many things are stored in each container in the classroom, or how many students can play on a piece of play equipment at any one time. Students could write new labels when the other labels need replacing. Ask: Which number do you need to write? Where can you find one to copy?

**Bingo**

Give students practice in recognising number symbols. To begin, students could use 'Bingo' cards that include the numbers 0 to 10. Gradually extend the numbers to include the 'teens' and 'decades' (e.g. 25, 52, 34, 43, 91, 19).

**Matching**

Organise students into pairs and have them play card games to match numbers to collections. For example, give each pair a set of cards. Half of the cards show different collections of between 0 and 10 things; the rest of the cards show a number between 0 and 9. The game ends when all the card pairs have been matched. Extend the numbers into the teens and beyond as students are ready.

**Next Number**

Ask students to read out loud the numbers on their calculators as they use the constant function to count. Stop students at 9, then ask: What number will be next? Check to see if you are correct. What is different about 9 and 10? Has the calculator used these single numbers before? Use students' responses to discuss the number of digits and the difference the place makes.

### Place-Value Beans

Invite students to count a handful of beans and record how many. Point to the digit representing the decade; for example, point to the 3 in 34 and ask students to find that number of beans. Focus on what the 3 in that place means. Repeat for the 4.

### Reach My Number

Ask students to make their own place-value kits. This kit includes: a sheet of A4 paper, which they rule into three columns, with headings (from left to right) 'Hundreds', 'Tens', 'Ones', and three sets of the digits 0-9 on card and collections of straws made up as singles and bundles of ten. Have students take turns to roll a ten-sided die or use a spinner to spin a number from 0 to 9 and use their place-value kits to keep score. When students reach the target number (e.g. 45), ask: How would the groups look if the number was 54? Which parts would be different?

### Expanded Notation

Invite students to read and record numbers as expanded notation (e.g. *28 is 2 tens and 8 ones*). Have them also write numbers from expanded notation shown in place value order as well as reversed order. Students should know that '8 ones and 2 tens' or '2 tens and 8 ones' are both 28.

**KU 5**

 **Did You Know?**

Many students are able to tell you which is the tens column and which is the ones column and can readily write 82 as 80 + 2. However, they may still have an uncertain grip on place value and don't really understand that the 8 in 82 means 8 tens. Such students often cannot sustain a place-value interpretation of numbers when confronted with non-standard groupings of the things. This is a key distinction between the Partitioning and Flexibility phases in students' understanding of how numbers work.

**Diagnostic Activity**

Ask a student to do the following activity. (Most students correctly write 26.) Point at the 2 and say: Use a red pen to show me this. Then, point at the 6 and say: Use a blue pen to show me this.

Look at the picture of cars and wheels.
How many wheels are there? _____

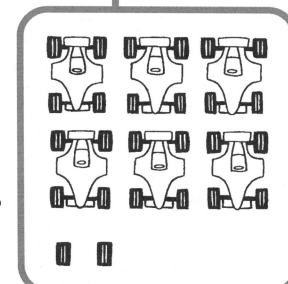

# SAMPLE LEARNING ACTIVITIES

## Middle ✔✔✔

### 100 Grid

Ask students to make their own 1 to 100 grid, arranging the numbers in whatever number of rows and columns they like. Have students use their grid to look for patterns in the numbers. Then, ask students to quickly find a number (e.g. 67 or 42). Show students a 10 x 10 grid and ask: What changes from one row to the next? Why? What changes in the other grids? Why? In which grid is it easiest to find particular numbers? Why? Have all students make a grid for their personal use. Encourage students to extend their grid over time. (See Reason About Number Patterns, Key Understanding 5.)

| 1 | 13 | 25 |
|---|----|----|
| 2 | 14 | 26 |
| 3 | 15 | 27 |
| 4 | 16 | |
| 5 | 17 | |
| 6 | 18 | |
| 7 | 19 | |
| 8 | 20 | |
| 9 | 21 | |
| 10 | 22 | |
| 11 | 23 | |
| 12 | 24 | |

| 1 | 2 | 3 | 4 | 5 | 6 |
|---|---|---|---|---|---|
| 7 | 8 | 9 | 10 | 11 | 12 |
| 13 | 14 | 15 | 16 | 17 | 18 |
| 19 | 20 | 21 | | | |
| | | | | | |

### Dice Rolls

Ask pairs of students to take turns to throw a die and record results in a row on squared paper, which is five squares wide. Have students choose which square to enter each digit in order to make the largest possible number. When both students have made a five-digit number, the player with the largest number chooses a different rule (e.g. *Make the lowest number or the number closest to 50 000*).

### Wipeout

Play with the whole class. Enter a number, such as 256, into the calculator. Ask: How can we make the 5 a zero? (*Subtract 50.*) Why did you do that? What number have we got now? Make the 2 a zero. Try larger numbers when students are ready. Later, have students play 'Wipeout' in pairs, taking turns to give each other the instructions. Encourage students to try larger numbers such as 946 256.

## Ten Times Greater

Organise students into pairs. Invite students to use their calculators to find out what is ten times greater than given numbers (e.g. 30, 172, 109, 200, 210, 4550). Ask: Can you see a pattern? Try to explain to your partner why that happens. What will 10 times 7568 be? Test it and see.

## Counting in Hundreds

Ask students to use constant addition on their calculator to count in 100s. Have them predict which number will come next, then press ▮ to verify. Ask: How many hundreds did you put in to make 900? How many hundreds are in 1000 (2000)?

## Multiplying by Ten

Have students predict the effect of multiplying a number by 10. Use the overhead projector calculator and begin with any single digit. Ask: If we multiply this number by 10, what will the number be? If we multiply by 10 again, what will the number be? How many tens in 100 (1000)?

## Three-Digit Numbers

Ask students to use grid paper to draw a diagram that shows the size of each of the digits in a three-digit number (e.g. 888). Ask: How do you know you have the size right for each of the digits? How much bigger is the second 8 than the first? Later, have students represent the size of the digits in other three-digit numbers (e.g. 256), without using grid paper.

## Marbles

Have students explain the meanings of the digits in a numeral using materials that are deliberately not grouped in standard ways—that is, not in tens (e.g. 26 marbles). For example, students put out six bags of four marbles and two more marbles. Ask: How many marbles? Have students write down how many. Record the correct answer on the board. Point to one digit and ask students to show their partner the number of marbles it refers to. Point to another digit and repeat. Repeat this activity with other collections that are not grouped in tens; for example, three bundles of ten popsticks and 13 singles.

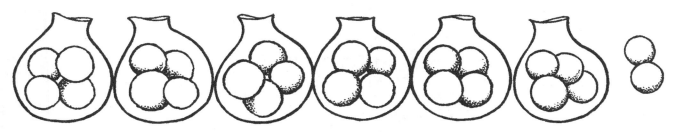

# SAMPLE LEARNING ACTIVITIES

## Later ✔✔✔

### 800 Game

Have students investigate the multiplicative relationship between places. Organise students into pairs. Then, give each student a card labelled '8' and up to five cards labelled '0'. Ask each student to make a different number with the digit cards. For example, the first student could make 8; the second student could make 800. Ask: What number sentence would you key into your calculator to change your number so that it is the same as your partner's? Have students share their number sentences, then ask: Who used addition and subtraction? Who used multiplication and division? Refer to a chart that shows the cyclical pattern of the number system to emphasise how multiplication and division match the relationship between the places. For example, say: To make 8 into 800, you can key 8 x 10 x 10 or 8 x 100 into your calculator. To make 800 into 8, you can key 800 ÷ 10 ÷ 10 or 800 ÷ 100 into your calculator. Have students repeat the activity making a different number with their cards and then use the chart to explain why the number sentence they chose actually works. Later, extend the activity to include a decimal point and more zeros.

### Counting Crowds

Have students solve problems such as: The number counter at the entrance to the show reads 9999 (10 999, 99 999) after the person in front of you went in. What will the counter read after you go in?

## Ten Times Smaller

Ask students to use their calculators to find out what is ten times smaller than each of these numbers: 30, 172, 109, 200, 210, 4550. Have them record their answers, then ask: What did you do? Did you need to do the same for each number? Repeat the activity with decimal numbers such as: 3, 2.1, 1.72, 1.09, 45.5. (See Key Understanding 7.)

## Dice Rolls

Have students make either the largest or the smallest number possible from a fixed number of dice rolls. They can use up to eight squares in a row to record a digit from each roll of the die. Each student has a 'free zero', which they can place anywhere in the row. After a few rounds, ask: What do you need to do to make the largest (smallest) number possible? Why?

## Million Square

Help students to create an area of one million square millimetres. Draw out the relationships between the powers of ten and successive places. Use millimetre grid paper and draw around 1 square millimetre, then 10, 100, 1000, 10 000 square millimetres and label. Combine cut-outs of 10 to 1000 square millimetres to create a million square. Ask: How much space do you think we'll need on the display board for this? (See Sample Lesson 4, page 82.)

## Changing Places

Ask students to use materials (e.g. MAB materials) to model the relationship between places. To begin, show students the smallest MAB block. Ask: What number is this? (*1*) Then, show the next largest base ten cube, and ask: What number is this? (*1000*) How much bigger is this than the first cube? (*1000 times bigger*) What do you think the next-sized cube will look like? Do you have enough large cubes in the school to build the next-sized cube? Do you have enough to build just the frame of the cube? Have students write the numbers for each cube. Say: Imagine what the fourth cube looks like. How do you say it?

## Words into Symbols

Have students rewrite large numbers written as words into symbols. Ask students to show all of the places. A good source for large numbers is newspapers; for example, 'The budget deficit is 8 billion.'

**KU 5**

## KEY UNDERSTANDING 6

*Place value helps us to think of the same whole number in different ways and this can be useful.*

This Key Understanding is closely linked to Key Understanding 2 because it is dependent on students' being able to think flexibly of numbers as being composed of other numbers. The idea is that we organise or group collections in various ways to make it easier to see how many there are. Groupings based on tens is the standard way to do this because we have chosen to build groupings of ten into the way we write numbers.

Students should develop the idea that the way we write numbers makes it easy to count forwards and backwards in tens, hundreds, and so on, as well as from any number. For example, counting forwards in tens from 17 (e.g. 17, 27, 37) is easy if you think about what must happen in the tens place rather than trying to add 10 each time. Students can develop a sense of how the tens shift along through activities, such as jumping along a written or imagined number line, or a line constructed from ten rods; dropping vertically down levels in a 1 to 100 chart; or adding tens in the form of 'longs' to numbers represented in MAB materials.

Place value makes it easy to split a number into parts. There are standard place-value partitions, such as $582 = 500 + 80 + 2$, but often non-standard partitions are more helpful. For example, thinking of 582 as $382 + 200$ helps us subtract 198.

Often, because place value is treated as a prerequisite to computation, students are taught to partition numbers before they can see a reason for doing so. However, the evidence suggests that place value should not be taught in isolation first. Rather, students should be challenged to use a variety of mental, diagrammatic and informal written strategies to work out calculations for themselves. (See also Calculate, Key Understandings 4, 5 and 6.)

This encourages students to use the patterns in the way we write and say numbers to split numbers into parts in helpful ways. This means that students develop place-value concepts simultaneously with calculation and as they need these concepts to calculate.

Students who have achieved Level 3 can partition whole numbers in standard ways, and two-digit numbers in non-standard ways. These students may be able to correctly partition 342 into 200 + __. Although, they do so by working out the 'sum' (e.g. *To get to 342 from 200, we have to add on a hundred and another 40 and 2*) rather than seeing it as flowing automatically from the values of the 'places'.

Students who have achieved Level 4 have developed flexibility with whole numbers. These students understand that multiple partitionings of the same number are possible and they are convinced that this does not change the original quantity. Furthermore, they use place value quickly and flexibly to partition larger whole numbers in order to facilitate their own computation and problem solving.

KU 6

## SAMPLE LEARNING ACTIVITIES

# Beginning ✔

### Grouping Objects

Have students count the number of objects in a container of materials, and record this number on a label that is kept with the materials. Where there are quantities over 100, ask students to group the objects in bags or bundles of ten to make the count easier. Then, have students write labels that say how many bags of 10s, 100s and singles are in the container. (Link to Calculate, Key Understanding 4.)

### Checking at a Glance

Store the class sets of glue, scissors, brushes, and so on, in rows of ten. Ask a student to check at a glance how many of each has been collected or needs to be collected. (Link to Calculate, Key Understanding 4.)

### Jigsaw Cards

Invite students to make sets of cards showing different representations of the same number. For example:

| 2 tens 3 ones |
|:-:|

| 1 ten 3 ones |
|:-:|

| 23 |
|:-:|

| twenty-three |
|:-:|

| ‖‖‖‖‖‖ ‖‖‖‖‖‖ ||| |
|:-:|

### Present or Absent

Have each student write their name in a box on a 10 x 4 grid as they arrive. Students can see at a glance how many are at school by checking the number of tens and ones on the grid.

### Arranging Collections

Ask groups of students to arrange a collection of objects (e.g. 43 matchsticks) in ways that make it easy to see how many there are. Students could use elastic bands, plastic bags or lids to arrange the objects. Have groups record, then compare, their arrangements. Focus on any arrangements using tens. Then, ask students to arrange a smaller collection (e.g. 32 matchsticks) so that it is easy to see how many there are.

## Place-Value Kits

Have students make their own place-value kits. On a sheet of A4 paper, students rule three columns and add the headings (from left to right) 'Hundreds', 'Tens', 'Ones'. Then, have them make three sets of 0 to 9 'place setting' cards, singles, bundles of tens and ten tens of straws.

| hundreds | tens | ones |
| --- | --- | --- |
| | | |

## Trading

Have pairs of students play trading games. They take turns to throw a die and take that many objects (e.g. beads) from a central bank. Then, students place the objects on their place-value kits and record a running total. Have students make groups of ten as they build on their totals. Each student tells their partner their new total and how it is arranged (e.g. *I have 24 beads. There are two tens and four ones.*)

## Number Sentences

Extend the 'Trading' activity by asking students to record each turn as a number sentence. Point to the digit in the tens column on their number sentence and ask them to show what that means in their collection. Have students build onto the large numbers by continuing from where they finished the previous game each time they play a new game. Vary the materials for each group of students and each new game.

$2 + 4 = 6$
$6 + 3 + 2 = 11$
$11 + 5 + 1 = 17$
$17 + 3 + 4 = 24$
$24 + 6 + 1 = 31$
$31 + 3 + 2 = 36$
$36$

## Who Has the Most?

Invite each student to take a handful of matchsticks and group the matchsticks into tens. Then, have them work with a partner to determine who has the most matchsticks by comparing the number of tens. Ask: If there are the same number of tens, what can you do now to find out who has the most? If one has more tens than the other, do you still need to count the ones?

KU 6

# SAMPLE LEARNING ACTIVITIES

## Middle ✔✔

### Teams

Discuss with students how to arrange three classes into teams so that the total number of students could be easily counted. Ask: Does groups of ten make it easier to count? Can you see groups of ten in other groups (e.g. 5s or 12s)?

### Regrouping

Have pairs of students decide who has the most matches. Each pair takes two handfuls of matches and groups them to make counting easier. Then, they count the matches before regrouping them in a different way and re-counting. Ask: Which grouping made it easier to count? Did you get the same number? Why? Why not? Is it easier to see 'how many' in the groups of three or groups of ten? Why?

### Counting On

Arrange some MAB materials, so there are some ones, some tens, then some more ones, more tens, and so on. Invite students to count on by 1s and 10s to say how many MAB cubes altogether. Cover the blocks with a piece of card and gradually uncover the materials as the count proceeds. Rearrange the cubes and ask students to re-count. Ask: Why is the total the same? Extend the activity to include 100s.

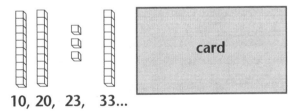

10, 20, 23, 33...

### Maths Methods

Present an operation horizontally on the board (e.g. 62 – 23). Allow time for students to calculate the answer in their heads, then ask them to explain what they did. Record different methods for calculating on the board and draw out how most methods break up the numbers. Ask: Why did you break the numbers up in that way? Why did you put those two numbers together first? (See Calculate, Key Understanding 4.)

### Trading

Organise students into groups of two to four. Have them play trading games with MAB materials and a ten-sided die, where, for example, 7 is worth 7 hundreds. Players collect their hundreds and trade into the thousands. At the end of a given period, students record their totals and say how many hundreds they have thrown. Ask students to count by hundreds to check.

### Backwards and Forwards

Have students use their 1 to 100 charts (see Key Understanding 4) to count forwards and backwards by 10s. Ask: What happens to the number in the tens place each time you move forwards (backwards)?

### Number Lines

Invite students to construct their own number lines to show the same movements as in the previous activity. Ask: At what number does your number line need to start? Does it need to show all of the numbers in between the counted numbers? Why? Why not?

### Breaking Up

Have students use materials grouped into tens (e.g. Unifix cubes, popsicle sticks, washers, MAB materials) to construct as many representations of a given number as possible. For example, *37* could be represented as *3 tens and 7 ones, 2 tens and 17 ones, 1 tens and 27 ones, or 37 ones*. Ask students to record their representations and justify each by showing how their groups of materials linked to the representations. Extend the activity to include three-digit numbers. (See Calculate, Key Understanding 2.)

### Word Problems

Ask students to solve word problems using standard and non-standard place-value groupings. For example, ask: What are the possible ways 45 sweets could be sold if they can be bought as singles or as rolls of ten? Have students illustrate the groups they make, and also use numbers to record the different ways; for example, 45 ones or 3 tens and 15 ones.

### Arranging Objects

Similar to the 'Word Problems' activity, have students work out the different ways they could buy 95 sweets if they come in boxes of 5, 10, 15, 20, 50. Ask students to record their ideas and select the arrangement of 95 sweets that they would prefer for their family. Have students represent and justify their choices.

KU 6

## SAMPLE LEARNING ACTIVITIES

### Later ✔✔✔

**Grouping Objects**

Ask students to work out all the different ways they could buy 795 sweets if the sweets come loosely as singles, boxes of 10, or packets of 10 boxes. Have students record the possible ways with diagrams and/or numbers and then later with numbers alone.

**Flexible Numbers**

Have standard and non-standard place-value partitions for two- or three-digit numbers (e.g. 61, 312, 454) on separate cards. Invite students to select and record the cards that can be used to represent each number. For example, for 312, they might select:

| 3 hundreds | 1 ten | 2 ones |
| 2 hundreds | 11 tens | 2 ones |
| 2 hundreds | 10 tens | 12 ones |

**Adding and Subtracting**

Have students add and subtract numbers by visualising a hundred chart. For example, show students a hundred chart for a few minutes and then remove it from view. Ask: What number is below 43? How do you know? What number is three to the right of 72? How do you know? You are at 34, go right two places and up three. Where are you now? You are at 68. How do you get to 75? Then, have students describe the jumps needed to calculate 24 + 39 and 83 − 47.

**Calculating**

Extend the 'Adding and Subtracting' activity by having students make up a thousand chart, with 1 to 100 along the top row, 101 to 200 on the second row, and so on. Ask similar questions as students use the chart to work out and explain their jumps.

**Leap Along a Number Line**

Have students make jumps of 1, 10 or 100 on a number line to calculate 423 + ? = 632, or 891 − 674 = ? (See Calculate, Key Understanding 2.)

## Different Strategies

Invite students to use partitioning and place value to solve problems mentally. Present students with a problem, such as: Your grandfather is 84, but you only have 67 candles. How many more do you need? Give students time to work the problem out in their heads and write down the answer. Ask: How did you do it? Write on the board the different ways students solved the problem. Discuss with students which methods they prefer and why.

## Partitioning Numbers

Have students work in pairs to partition numbers to help them do calculations. For example, to calculate 99 x 27, students might see 99 as 100 – 1 and think, *That's one hundred 27s less one 27,* so jot down:  2700
                                                           – 27

To calculate 4 x 27, students might think, *Four lots of 20 and four lots of 7,* and jot down the partial products on paper:  80
                                                    + 28

Later, for 34 x 27, students might think, *That's thirty 27s add four 27s,* leading to something like the standard algorithm.

## Grid Partitions

Invite students to explore ways of breaking up numbers for multiplication calculations. For example, represent 16 x 14 using grid paper and find an easy way of breaking up the grid to help work out the total. Then, ask students to share the various partitions and decide which ones make calculating easier.

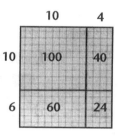

## Decimals

Have students use 2 mm grid paper, with a 10 x 10 square representing one whole, to represent and calculate with decimals. For example, to calculate 6 x 3.3, a student might draw around the squares showing 6 lots of 3.3 and show that 6 x 3 = 18 and write 18. 6 x 3 tenths is 1 and 8 tenths that's 1.8. Add 18 + 1 + 0.8 to reach a total of 19.8. Invite students to compare the different ways they used the grid to break up the numbers to work it out.

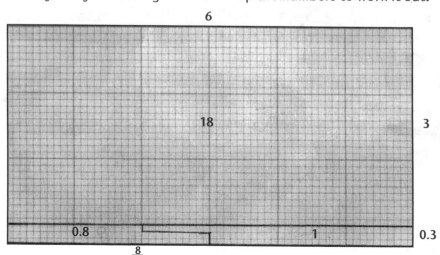

KU 6

## KEY UNDERSTANDING 7

### *We can extend the patterns in the way we write whole numbers to write decimals.*

Students may develop their initial ideas about decimals from using a calculator and from dealing with money and measurements. They will readily accept that the calculator shows 'a half' as 0.5, and use the decimal point in the way we write money and measures. However, it is important that students develop an understanding of the structure and relationships involved when place value is extended to represent decimal numbers.

Partitioning into smaller and smaller units multiplicatively (each partitioning is one-tenth of the previous one) is considerably more difficult than grouping into larger and larger units. Understanding the pattern in the sequence $1, \frac{1}{10}, \frac{1}{100}, \frac{1}{1000}$ is central in understanding decimal notation. Students should have many experiences designed to help them develop the following ideas.

- There are numbers between consecutive whole numbers.

- The place-value system can be extended to the right of the units place to show numbers between two whole numbers.

- To represent a number between two consecutive whole numbers, record the smaller whole, followed by the part, separated by a decimal point (e.g. a number between 4 and 5 is 4.67).

- The digits to the right of the unit have decreasing values in powers of ten with the first place representing tenths, the second hundredths, and so on, and can represent infinitely small numbers.

- Decimal fractions can be partitioned just as whole numbers can (e.g. 0.74 is 0.7 + 0.04 , 0.30 + 0.44, $\frac{7}{10} + \frac{4}{100}$, $\frac{74}{100}$ and $\frac{740}{1000}$).

Students who have achieved Level 3 of the outcome are able to 'read' money and measures as a whole number and 'some more'. These students may, however, think of the decimal point as simply a way of separating the dollars and cents, or the metres and centimetres. They may not understand how place value works.

*(handwritten notes in margin: "Focus points", "go in both directions", "diagnostic chart (phases)")*

Students who have achieved Level 4 can rewrite the decimal part of a number as a fraction (e.g. 0.35 is $\frac{35}{100}$). They can also name the first few places and say that 0.35 is $\frac{3}{10} + \frac{5}{100}$. However, students may not be able to use the multiplicative relationship between the places to move flexibly between these forms. They should develop flexibility in their partitioning of decimal numbers, since different forms of representation are helpful in different situations.

At Level 5, students understand the link between 0.35 being $\frac{35}{100}$ and also $\frac{3}{10} + \frac{5}{100}$. They can flexibly partition decimal numbers in multiple ways; for example, knowing that 0.36 is 0.3 + 0.06 and also 0.2 + 0.16, and so on. These students are fully operational in their use of decimal place value.

### ? Did You Know?

Year 7 and 8 students solved a money problem and got 6.125 on their calculators. Many students then 'rounded' this figure to $7.25, thinking that the decimal point separates the number of dollars from the number of cents (i.e. six dollars and 125 cents). This is a common error.

Students who make this mistake may be making good sense of what they hear because the general rule about the way we say the decimal places is ignored for money. For example, we say $45.27 as 'forty-five dollars, twenty-seven'. Students need to learn that money uses decimal 'logic' even though we do not always say it that way. The decimal places actually refer to parts of a dollar.

KU 7

## SAMPLE LEARNING ACTIVITIES

# Beginning ✔

### Half

During fraction activities, ask students to divide 1 by 2 on their calculators to see 0.5 as another way of representing a half.

### Counting by 0.5

Have students count by 0.5 on their calculator and then record the sequence as a number line.

### Dollars and Cents

Ask students to focus on the decimal point as the separator between the dollars and parts of a dollar. For example, sit students in a circle with money they have brought to school. Help each student say how much money they have and write that amount on the board. Select students to identify each part of the written amount, ask: Where did you put the decimal point? Why is it there? What part of your number means the dollars (parts of a dollar)?

### Price Tags

Invite students to write price labels for class shop, including prices that require five cents, fifty cents and fifty-five cents (e.g. $4.05, $4.50, $4.55). Ask: Is five cents written the way you would expect it to be? Which one of your price tags did you have to think about the hardest? What does the 5 mean in each of the tags? Which of these prices is the dearest?

### Skip Counting Money

Ask students to skip count, forwards and backwards, by five cents (ten cents), up to and over one dollar. Then, ask them to skip count by one dollar (five, ten dollars), up to and over 100.

### Age Groups

Have students enter their ages on to their calculators, then organise themselves into groups according to the number shown on their calculators. Ask: What does your 5 (6, 7, 8) mean? Who is exactly 5 (6, 7, 8) years old? Who is more than 6 years old, but not 7 years old? Can you show this on the calculator? Look for a response that can be developed into writing their ages as, for example, 6.5 or 6.75. Encourage language, such as: *I'm six and a bit*. Write students' exact ages in order on the board. Have students regroup into those age groups.

## SAMPLE LEARNING ACTIVITIES

# Middle ✔✔

### Peg Up

Hang a piece of line or string and peg up two cards: one labelled '0' on the left and one labelled '4' on the right. Invite students to say where cards labelled 1, 2 and 3 should go on the line. Then, show 2.5 and ask: Where should this number be placed? Peg it on the line when students answer correctly. Ask: What does 2.5 mean? Are there other numbers like this that we could put up on the line? Have students write the numbers (*0.5, 1.5, 3.5*) and add them to the line. Encourage students to explain why they have placed their number on a particular part of the line.

### Tenths

Have students estimate, then place fraction cards on the 'Peg Up' line to show $\frac{0}{10}$ through to $\frac{10}{10}$. Help them to rename the fractions as decimals.

### Larger Decimals

Extend 'Peg Up' to include larger numbers; for example, 35, 35.2, 35.4, 36.1, 36.2, and so on, through to 41.9.

### Writing Fractions as Decimals

Ask students to make a metre rule with every 10 centimetres marked. Then, have them use this rule to measure lengths to the nearest 10 centimetres. Invite students to record these lengths in metres and fractions of a metre. Show them how to write tenths as a decimal (e.g. 0.1). Ask: What is another name for 0.1 (1.1)? What does the zero mean when we write 0.3?

### Number Scrolls

Have students use constant addition on their calculators to count by a decimal, such as 0.2, and record the numbers as they go. When they reach 0.8, ask: What comes next? Invite students to push ▪ to verify, then ask: Is the answer what you expected? Discuss any conflicts. Then, ask students to continue, first predicting, then checking answers. Students could then count by fifths to make the link between decimals and fractions.

### Counting by Decimals

Ask students to use the constant function to count by 0.5 and then 0.25. Students could then represent both sequences on one number line and say why some numbers are in both sequences.

# SAMPLE LEARNING ACTIVITIES

## Later ✔✔✔

### Counting by Decimals

Have students use the constant function on their calculators to count by 0.2. Ask them to read and list each number as it appears on the display. Stop students at 1.8 and invite them to predict what the next number will be. Have students check to verify their predictions. Ask: Why can't the next number after 1.8 be 1.10? Then, ask students to continue the count to 2.8. Repeat the predict-and-check cycle through 3.8, 4.8, and so on. Select students to say the number sequence forwards and backwards.

### Decimal Number Line

Hang a long piece of string across the classroom. Set up a decimal number line, with a card labelled '2' on the extreme left of the line and a card labelled '3' on the extreme right. Write '2.5' on another card and ask where it should go. When students answer correctly, peg the number card in position on the line. Ask students to write another number to add to the line and to explain why they have placed their card in that position. Later, extend the activity to thousandths and decimals with different numbers of places.

### Place Invaders

Extend 'Wipeout' (see Key Understanding 5, Middle Sample Learning Activities), so that numbers can only be wiped out from the ones place. Discuss with the students how they may need to multiply by 10s (if tenths are present) or 100s (if two decimal places) to remove the decimal first. For example, for the number 256.37, multiply the number by 100 to make 25637 and then subtract 7. Ask: How do you know what to multiply or divide by to get the digit into the ones place?

### Packs

Ask students to use an extended place-value table that includes decimal places. (See Key Understanding 4.)

| hundreds | tens | ones | hundreds | tens | ones | tenths | hundredths | thousandths |
|---|---|---|---|---|---|---|---|---|
| | thousands | | | ones | | • | fractions | |
| 3 | 4 | 6 | 4 | 2 | 7 | • 1 | 2 | 5 |

Recount a story about an office that uses an average of 1.23 packs of paperclips each month. Given that each pack has 10 boxes of 100 paperclips, have students decide how many paperclips the office uses on average. Ask: Does this seem reasonable? Point to the individual digits in 1.23 and ask how many paperclips each digit represents.

## Recording Measurements

Ask students to decide what the decimal point shows when using it to record measures, such as their height, or how high and how long they can jump. Have students record each measurement in centimetres (132 cm), metres and centimetres (1 m, 32 cm), and metres (1.32 m). Ask: What does the 1 in 1.32 mean? What does the decimal point do? What does the 'point three two' mean? Focus on the decimal point separating metres from parts of a metre.

## Decimal Fractions

Use decimetre squares of 1 millimetre grid paper as units to show how successive division by 10 relates to the places. Cut the grid paper into ten pieces, take one-tenth and write 0.1; cut that piece into ten pieces and take one-tenth, then write 0.01, and so on. Cut a square into two pieces, keeping to grid lines, and calculate the decimal fraction of each piece. Ask: If you are using a calculator to add the two numbers together, why must the result be 1?

## Ordering Measurements

Invite students to order a series of measurements in metres (litres, kilograms) and say what the digits to the right of the decimal point mean. Perhaps these figures could be taken from the jumps and throws recorded at a recent sports carnival. Then, ask questions, such as: Which is longer 2.34 or 2.5? Why? How many centimetres is 2.5 metres? (See Key Understanding 3.)

## Lengths as Decimals

Ask students to record lengths as decimals on a metre ruler. Ask: If we need to be more accurate than measuring to the nearest 10 centimetres, how could we make smaller measures on our ruler? Focus attention on splitting a tenth into tenths and renaming these as hundredths. Ask students what fractional part of the metre each place represents. For example, ask: What does the first place after the decimal point represent? What does the second (third) place represent?

KU 7

## KEY UNDERSTANDING 8

### *We can compare and order the numbers themselves.*

Although numbers can be applied in all sorts of different ways in the real world, they are also abstract objects that can be thought about and manipulated in their own right. Moving backwards and forwards between quantities and abstract numbers can help us to make sense of each.

However, enabling students to think of numbers independently of any particular context is the essence of this Key Understanding. We can think of 'three' separately from three things. Without having to refer to physical objects or actual quantities, we can compare and order the numbers themselves. We know that 8 is one more than 7, 3.5 is halfway between 3 and 4, −4 is less than 0, and 1000 is ten times as big as 100. We also think of numbers as having a magnitude: 3 is a small number and 3 000 000 is a big number. Although we express this in absolute terms, we are implicitly making relative or comparative statements. Compared to 3, 300 is a big number; compared to 3 000 000, 300 is a small number. Students should have many experiences that help them to get a sense of the order and relative magnitude of numbers.

At times, there may be conflict between the way we deal with the numbers as abstractions and the way we deal with them in the real world. The number 200 is always bigger than the number 30 and we might even think of 200 as a 'big' number. But an annual rainfall of 200 millimetres is very low (it is about what the towns of Kalgoorlie and Broken Hill get), while a rainfall of 30 inches is moderate (it is about what Perth, Melbourne and London get). This apparent conflict is caused because 200 and 30 as numbers only make sense in relation to the same unit, the number 1. Students need the opportunity to talk through such ambiguities.

Students should learn to think of numbers as positioned on a number line and so use a range of calibrated scales. Initially, they should imagine moving backwards and forwards on a number line, often in conjunction with counting forwards and backwards on a calculator. Later, the focus should be on the relative order and size of numbers written as decimals. Students should 'count' in decimal fractions (e.g. 0.2, 0.4, 0.6, 0.8) using both a number line and a calculator to generate and check their counts. They should learn to read a range of scales including where the number of marks between the units may be 10 or 5 or 20.

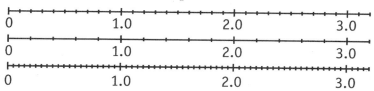

Students who have achieved Level 2 think of the numbers within their counting range separately from real objects; the numbers alone carry the meaning. These students understand the significance of the order when it is used to count things, knowing that you can tell from the numbers alone which collection has more (see Key Understanding 1).

At Level 3, students can think of whole numbers beyond their practical counting experience as having a relative magnitude and order independently of any particular context. They make and use whole number lines to assist in their computation.

At Level 4, students' understanding of place value means that they readily make order of magnitude comparisons between whole numbers (see Key Understanding 5). They understand decimals as numbers, rather than as ways of representing measures or money. These students can also place decimal numbers (e.g. 0.2, 0.4, 0.6, 0.8. 1.0. 1.2) on a number line and read scales, including some instances where every calibration is not marked.

At Level 5, students order decimals, including when the number of places is unequal. They can also read a wide range of scales involving decimals.

KU 8

## SAMPLE LEARNING ACTIVITIES

### Beginning ✔

#### Number Sequences

Ask students to enter a number between 1 and 30 on their calculators. Organise students into small groups. Ask each group to order themselves, from the greatest number displayed to the lowest number. Then, have two small groups combine and repeat the process. Combine groups again and repeat. When two large groups remain, ask one group to read its sequence. Ask students in the second group to think about where their numbers will fit in the first sequence, before combining the groups to form one sequence. Discuss with students the need to deal with the situation where numbers are doubled up or tripled.

#### Counting Forwards

Invite students to use the constant function on their calculators to count forwards by 1s. Ask: Why does 9 come after 8 and not before it?

#### Negative Numbers

Ask students how they might get their calculators to count backwards. Have students begin at a chosen number number (e.g. 20) and record the numbers as they are displayed. When students reach 5, ask: What's happening to the numbers? Have students predict what will happen after they reach 1. Ask: Do you think you can keep going? Try it. What's happening to the numbers now? Have you seen this kind of number before?

#### Number Line

Have students record the numbers in the 'Negative Numbers' activity as a number line.

#### Forward and Reverse

Invite students to play 'Forward and Reverse' to develop an imagined number line. This game can be played by either the whole class or in groups. Have the leader count forwards by ones/clap slowly while the other students imagine counting forwards along a number line each time the leader claps. After several claps, the leader stops the count so students can say what number they are at. Vary the game by using signals to change to counting backwards. The leader can decide when to change the direction of the counting. Later, the leader can direct the students to change from counting by ones to skip counting by 5s (10s) by giving a unit of say three claps, then repeating it for each jump.

**Peg Up**

Hang a piece of string across the classroom. Ask each student to write any number on a card. Select one student to peg their card on the number line. Then, invite the rest of the class to determine whether their number is larger or smaller and, in turn, add their number card to the line. As more numbers are added to the line, students will need to decide whether the position of some of the cards has to be changed in order to get the sequence right. Over time, have students add more numbers to the line as they arise. For example, ask: How old is your grandfather? Where can we add that number to the line?

### Did You Know?

A calibrated scale is simply a part of a number line. When we use number lines in school, we usually tell the students the number and they find the place on the number line whereas with a real world calibrated scale you usually have to decide what the number is. This often involves estimating because the thing being measured will not exactly match a marked line. Students find this quite difficult.

Draw the number lines below on the board. Ask students to decide what number is indicated by each arrow.

| 0 | ↑ ↑ | 100 |
|---|---|---|
| 9 | ↑ ↑ | 10 |
| 0 | ↑ ↑ | 1 |
| 100 ↑ ↑ | | 300 |

| 0 ↑ ↑ | | 0.1 |
|---|---|---|
| 0 ↑ ↑ | | 5.0 |
| 0 ↑ ↑ | | 0.5 |
| 1 ↑ ↑ | | 3 |

KU 8

## SAMPLE LEARNING ACTIVITIES

### Middle ✔✔

#### Peg Up

Ask students to select a number between 0 and 1000 and write it on a piece of card. Have students peg their cards in order on a line strung across the classroom. Ask students to write another card that fits between their card and the next card. When faced with fitting a card between, for example, 37 and 38, students might say 37.5 or 37.75. Ask: How do you know the numbers are in the correct position? How do you know which is bigger?
(See Key Understanding 7.)

#### Correct Order

Have students choose a number and enter it in their calculator. Then, ask students to place themselves in order around the room from lowest to highest number. Have students call out their numbers in turn to show they are in the correct order.

#### Skip Counting

Ask students to make a number line with numbers from 0 to 200, or more. Have students mark every ten with a heavier line. Then, invite students to choose any beginning number and count in 10s. Ask: What patterns do you see? What happens if you skip count by 20s?

#### Estimating

Have students turn their number line from the 'Skip Counting' activity face down so they cannot see the numbers. Then, ask them to place a blank strip of tape underneath the number line with 1 marked. Have students choose a number and estimate where it will be on the number line, then mark the spot on the tape. Invite students to turn over the marked number line and check. Repeat the process, using the feedback to help students improve their estimating skills.

#### Number Scrolls

Ask students to count by 0.2 using the constant function on their calculators. Have them read, then record, the numbers from the display. Stop at 0.8 and ask students to predict the next number. Have students verify, then predict again, at 2.8, 3.8, 4.8, and so on. Ask students to read the sequence forwards and backwards. Ask: What number is before 3.2? What comes after 5? What is 0.4 bigger than 6.8? (Link to Key Understanding 7 and Middle Sample Learning Activity, Key Understanding 4.)

**Skip Counting Backwards**

Ask students to select a small number and use it to skip count along a number line for ten jumps. Then, have students count backwards for 15 jumps. Ask: What happened after zero? What happens to the numbers if you continue skip counting backwards?

**Temperatures**

Have students look in the weather section of a newspaper and record the maximum or minimum winter temperatures of a city over a five-day period. Ask students to plot the numbers on a number line. Ask: Where should zero be on the line? Why? Which is colder: 38 °C or – 3 °C (– 3 °C or – 5 °C)? Which is bigger: – 3 or – 5?

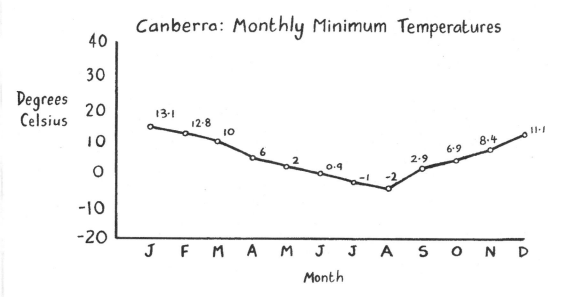

Canberra: Monthly Minimum Temperatures

**Biggest Number**

Invite students to circle the biggest number in each of the following groups and to explain their reasoning.

78, 87

109, 119, 190

1230, 1032, 1302

21.4, 24.1, 42.1, 41.2

KU 8

## SAMPLE LEARNING ACTIVITIES

### Later ✔✔✔

**Decimal Number Line**

Have students place decimal numbers between consecutive whole numbers on a number line. For example, ask students to find five numbers between 37 and 38 and then place them in approximate position. Invite students to say how they know one number comes before another. (See Key Understanding 7.)

**Calibrated Scales**

On an overhead projector, show a drawing of a measuring jug containing liquid. Place a scale on it, showing five calibrations between each whole number of millilitres. Ask students to record how much liquid is in the measuring jug. Then, remove the scale and replace it with one that has ten calibrations between each millilitre. Ask students again to record how much liquid there is. Some students are likely to have written different numbers (e.g. 1.3 for five gradations and 1.6 for ten gradations). Ask: Can both answers be right? Use the conflict between answers to generate discussion of the meaning of the gradations. For the five gradations scale, the calibrations jump by 0.2. Repeat the activity for 20 calibrations.

**Tenths**

Provide students with a number line (graduated scale) marked in tenths and ask them to place the numbers 1.5, 1.05, 1.50. Use an overhead projector to show various decisions on a scale calibrated in tenths. Have students discuss in small groups which answers are right and how they might check. Overlay a scale calibrated in hundredths to help students make their choice. Ask students report conclusions about the role of zero in different positions.

**Decimal Sequences**

Have students predict the next two terms in one of these sequences: 1.2, 1.4, 1.6, 1.8; or 1.97, 1.98, 1.99. Record students' answers on the board. (Note: Some students may predict 1.10 as the next number in the sequence for the first example.) Ask students to use the constant function on their calculators to check. Organise students into groups. Have each group work out what thinking led to each response and to decide what is the right thinking. Then, ask students to generate their own 'tricky sequences' for partners to try and then check on a calculator or number line.

### More Than/Less Than

Ask students to work with a partner to compare their explanations about the order of numbers and then decide whether they are correct. Invite students to explain what is wrong with explanations, such as these: *0.038 > 0.2 because 38 is more than 2; 8.05257 > 8.514 because it has more places; 17.353 < 17.35 because when you change them into fractions $\frac{35}{100}$ is bigger than $\frac{353}{1000}$.*

### Changing Values

Invite students to use the relationship between the places in a number to change the value of a digit. For example, say: Key in 4 on your calculators. Change 4 to 4000. What is the easiest way? Then, change 4000 to 40. How did you do it? What is the easiest way? Change 40 to 0.4.

### Graduated Number Lines

Provide students with three number lines marked from 1 to 3, graduated into fifths, tenths and twentieths respectively. Ask students to mark 1.2 on each number line. Say: Now, place the number lines under each other. What do you find? Are your numbers lined up? Should they be? Discuss in groups. Then, ask students to place 1.5, 1.05 and 1.50 on their number lines.

### Ordering Numbers

Have students order numbers in groups, such as:

- 0.6, $\frac{6}{100}$, 6.0

- 340 000 000; 34 000 000; 3 million, 4 hundred thousand; 34 000; 3 billion, 400 million.

Invite students to explain their reasoning.

### Negative Numbers

Provide students with a range of frozen food packs. Ask them to make a list, then place in order, all the negative numbers. Ask: Which is the lowest temperature? How do you know? Show this on a number line.

### Million Square

Help students create an area of one million square millimetres, drawing out the quantitative relationships between the powers of ten and successive places. Use one-millimetre grid paper and draw around 1, then 10, 100, 1000, 10 000 square millimetres and label. Combine cut-outs of 10 000 square millimetres to create a million square. Ask: How much space on the display board do you think we'll need for this? (See Sample Lesson 4, page 82.)

KU 8

## SAMPLE LESSON 4

**Sample Learning Activity:** Later—'Million Square', pages 59 and 81

**Key Understanding 8:** We can compare and order the numbers themselves.

**Focus:** The relative magnitude of whole numbers

**Working Towards:** Levels 3 and 4

### Teacher's Purpose

Many of my Year 7 students could read and write numerals beyond 1000, but I didn't think they had a real sense of the size of the numbers involved. I wanted them to see the relative increase in magnitude with each place.

### A Challenge

I gave each student a sheet of one-millimetre grid paper. Then, I challenged them to draw around 1000 tiny squares in 30 seconds. Most students grouped and counted. A few students successfully completed the activity in the time allowed. I asked the students to explain their strategies and focused on those students who had seen that a 10 x 10 square had 100 units and ten of those made 1000.

**I'm counting by 25's.**

**I'm counting how many across the page, then down in rows till I get to a thousand.**

**10 squares**

I knew the 10 x 10 square is 100, so it was just a strip of 10 squares.

### Extending the Challenge

The students were then asked to draw around one million squares. A few students knew that it could not be done on the page provided. Most students began to calculate how many squares on the page to see if there were, in fact, one million or more.

Several students could say how many squares were on the page and could explain how they knew this was less than one million. However, none could say whether there would be more than one million squares on two, three, or five pages. I told the class that to find out we would need to construct a sheet of grid paper that contained exactly one million squares. The students were also asked to think about whether or not I'd left enough space on the notice board for one million square millimetres. The students' ideas varied widely, but everyone thought there would be enough space.

## Opportunity to Learn

The next part of the activity was directed because I wanted the students to follow the pattern as it developed. First, I asked the students to draw around a single tiny square in the top left-hand corner of their grid paper and label it '1'. Then, I asked them to draw around ten squares in a column down the page, including the first square. I drew students' attention to the way we write 'one' and 'zero' to indicate the ten tiny squares.

Next, I asked students to draw around the column and another nine across the page, then label it '100'. I asked students to explain how they knew it was 100. Some students mentioned MAB units, longs and flats. I drew out that knowing ten times ten is one hundred was sufficient to convince ourselves absolutely that there were one hundred tiny squares without having to count them one by one. Then, I asked students to extend the squares down the page so that they drew around a bigger strip of ten 'hundred squares'.

I posed a series of questions. 'How many hundreds have we got now? How do we show this with a numeral? Can you explain how this fits in with our pattern so far? How is this different from the MAB 1000?'

Then, I directed the students to extend the row across the page so that we had now enclosed the number of tiny squares there were in ten of the 'thousand rows'. We talked about how the quantity and the numeral were linked for ten thousand (10 000) in the same way they were for ten ones (10), ten tens (100) and ten hundreds (1000).

## Connection and Challenge

'Now, do you think our class has enough "ten thousand squares" to make up the million tiny squares we'd planned?' I asked.

Many students said, 'Of course, we must have!' Meanwhile, some students frowned and started to calculate 29 x 10 000.

We continued the pattern to construct a strip of ten, ten thousands. Again, I asked the same question, 'How many in the strip?'

'There were ten "ten thousand squares", so that's one hundred thousands, because ten tens are one hundred,' was the response. We wrote 100 000.

After finishing the final ten rows, the students were excited to realise that there *had to be* one million tiny squares in ten rows of a hundred thousand, even though we'd not actually counted them. Everyone was impressed by the size of the square. To draw out the pattern further, we also listed the multiplication by tens relationship we'd worked through.

KU 8

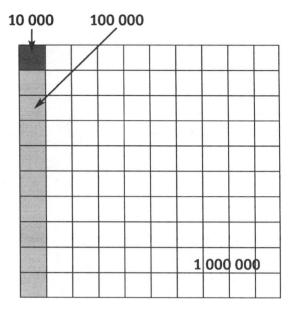

10 000    100 000

1 000 000

In this giant square of grid paper, there are one million (1 000 000) tiny squares.

1 (1 in the ones place)

10 x 1 = 10 (1 in the tens place)

10 x 10 = 100 (1 in the hundreds place)

10 x 100 = 1000 (1 in the thousands place)

10 x 1000 = 10 000 (1 in the ten thousands place)

10 x 10 000 = 100 000 (1 in the hundred thousands place)

10 x 100 000 = 1 000 000 (1 in the millions place)

If we cut the square into millimetre strips then it would stretch out for a thousand metres. Hey, that would be a kilometre! A kilometre is a million millimetres.

Now ten million would be a huge strip that was ten of those across the wall, but you'd need a much bigger wall, and a hundred million would be ten of those strips. We'd need to go out in the quadrangle to stick a hundred million together.

## Teacher's Comments

*I think the power of using 'area' to represent the number system is that the relative quantity of square millimetres was really emphasised as we built up the 'times ten' pattern for each place. In particular, the difference between the thousand, which was only a one-centimetre by ten-centimetre strip, and the square metre 'million' made a real impact.*

*With MAB materials, the values can be deceiving because the 1000 cube doesn't really show all the little cubes or look that big. Some students think of it as 100 cubes for each face (600).*

## Connecting and Extending

Later in the year, students were asked to think about counting one-metre squares instead of one-millimetre squares.

'What number would we then write to represent one of the tiny squares?' I wondered.

I then worked down from the new unit, in tenths, hundredths, and so on, so students would see that for decimal fractions, the same pattern of place-value relationships held, and there were also logical patterns in the way the numerals were written. This relates to Key Understanding 6 in this chapter, as well as Key Understanding 6 in Understand Units in the Measurement strand.

# BACKGROUND NOTES

## *Linking Counting to 'How Many?'*

Generally, children learn to use the number names one, two and three through a range of family and cultural practices as the number words are used almost as an adjective in the same way that the word 'blue' is used to describe 'blue shoes'. The idea of number begins to emerge as children recognise pairs of things. They learn to name pairs of things as 'two' perhaps by pointing and saying 'two eyes', 'two ears' and comparing this with only 'one nose'. In a similar way, through familiar rhymes and stories, they learn to recognise and name three things at a glance: 'three pigs', 'three blind mice', etc.

## The emergent linking of quantity with number names

As the idea of 'oneness', 'twoness' and 'threeness' emerges, children develop the concept of number. They recognise that the numbers 'one', 'two' and 'three' are alike (they all represent 'set size' or quantity) and yet they are also different (they represent different set sizes or quantities).

Most children can relate small numbers to each other without actually counting. They 'know' that two is more than one even if they do not have the language to describe that knowledge. Being able to express the basic idea that a collection of two (always) has more than a collection of one, that a collection of three always has more than a collection of two, and so on, is the basis for ordering those numbers and, hence, for connecting them with the counting sequence, 1, 2, 3, ...

Trying to teach children to use the number names to 'count' a collection is likely to be unsuccessful if they are unable to see the difference in size between small collections or have not learned to use the number words 'one', 'two' and 'three' to name the difference in size. This would be like trying to teach children to read before they know what books are for.

For many children, the capacity to distinguish small quantities and to use the first few counting numbers to name those quantities develops before they begin school. Therefore, it is easy to overlook its significance. However, some children, particularly those with intellectual delay or disability, may not develop this capacity as early or readily. Such children will need experiences in the early years that focus explicitly on learning to distinguish small quantities and use the first few counting numbers to name the quantities. Without this learning experience, they may then learn to count in a technical sense but may not be able to make sense of the process and, consequently, they will not learn to use counting to answer questions.

## Children's early experience of numbers

In many families, learning to recite the number names in order is the focus of many informal and playful activities. Other activities are focused on counting actions — steps, spoonfuls, jumps and pointing fingers at objects. Children, at first, imitate and coordinate the actions and words of counting and, only over an extended period, learn to see that this tells them 'how many' things there are.

In order to systematically count a collection, children need both to remember the counting sequence and know how to use the sequence in one-to-one correspondence with the items in the collection. However, the order in which children learn these two things will vary (just as some children learn many separate words before they attempt to say a whole sentence while other children rarely say an individual word before they suddenly speak a whole sentence).

One child may recite the number names correctly up to 40 or 50 or even more and yet may not be able to reliably count 8 or 9 things unassisted. This child needs to learn the counting process, that is, how to *use* the number names one-to-one to count a collection (as described in Key Understanding 1). Another child may only remember the number names to ten or twelve but may be able to use these numbers one-to-one to decide how many there are in a collection of 8 or 9 items. This child probably does not need to learn *how* to count a collection, but needs help to *remember* more of the number sequence so he or she can extend the repertoire to which they can apply their understanding of the counting process (as described in Key Understanding 4).

In each of the above scenarios, children use the sequence of the numbers to count how many are in a collection. It seems like 'common sense'; if you cannot 'count' to 8 (in the sense of saying the number names in order), you will not be able to 'count' a collection of 8 objects and this is often assumed in the way that teaching and testing programs are sequenced.

Learning to recite the numbers in order is not equally valued in all families. For example, some Aboriginal communities may find reciting sequences of number out of context to be an odd thing to do and not teach their children counting songs and games. However, this does not necessarily mean that children are not encouraged to develop a sense of number, since other social activities may help children recognise 'how many' are in a scattered collection just by looking at it. In some Aboriginal communities, subitizing is the focus of informal and playful activities. These activities are different from, but parallel to the counting oriented activities experienced by many children from majority cultures. Such children may not 'count', in the sense that they are unable to say the numbers in order up to eight or nine, but have learned to tell that there are six birds flying overhead or there are seven lollies on the table. They recognise 'sixness' in the same way that other children recognise 'threeness'.

For these children, learning to count may require that they investigate collections by recognising that they may have 'five' or 'six' or 'seven' things in each collection, then comparing and equalising quantities and talking about what they have done. These children should be able to place these collections in order so that each collection is bigger than the one before it. This is the basis for understanding why we say the numbers 5, 6, 7 ... in the counting sequence in that order: each number in the sequence is one more than the one before.

## Sequencing learning activities to link quantity with the order of the number names

The fact that we want children to achieve a common learning outcome does not mean that they should all experience the same activities or curriculum, sequenced in the same way; in fact, the opposite is preferred. As indicated above, all children are different and will come to school with varied experiences.

Some children may begin by knowing the counting sequence and need to learn to use it to work out 'how many'. Other children may begin by seeing 'how many' and then need to learn the counting sequence from it. Neither order is better or preferable. However, if the questions we ask children and the way we sequence learning activities assumes that learning 'naturally' proceeds in the way it does for the majority of Australian children, then we are likely to place the minority of children whose learning sequence may be different at an educational risk.

We might imagine some children living in place A and others living in place B, all have to get to a third place C. We can provide each with the best pathway to C, or we can require those who live at A to travel to B and then take the path from B to C. If we do the latter,

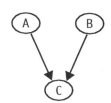

Optimal (but different) pathway for child A and B

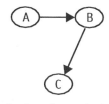

Optimal pathway designed for child B and child A is expected to catch up and follow it.

then the children who start at A clearly have farther to go. Is it any wonder they fall behind? In an analogous way, a 'common' input curriculum *may* cause educational disadvantages.

In such cases, the risk does not lie in a specific characteristic of the children or their backgrounds but rather in the inappropriate match of the curriculum to their knowledge. Thus, we may not recognise that the children *can* tell 'how many'; we, therefore, think of them as 'falling link behind' and move them through the learning pathways that is familiar and comfortable to *us* rather than those pathways that will be the most helpful for their learning.

By failing to respect and build upon their existing strategies, we actually undermine these children. The challenge is to ensure that the more popular developmental sequences known by the majority of children do not dominate and therefore become the mechanism by which certain children are *put* at educational risk rather than the means by which educational risk is reduced or removed. We *do* want children to learn to link the counting sequence to quantity but they do not all have to learn this in the same way or order. Children do not all have to make the same journey; rather we want to them all to arrive at the same destination.

Most children are likely to learn 'to count' in the sense of chanting the number names in order and *then* learn to count a collection by 1-1 matching of the number names in order with the items. Others may learn to recognise 'how many' are in small collections by looking, that is, they may recognise 'sixness' before they can chant number names in order to six. Either way, the two ideas must come together so that children see the link between the order in which we say the number names and the size of collections.

# CHAPTER 4

# Understand Fractional Numbers

This chapter will support teachers in developing teaching and learning programs that relate to this outcome:

> *Read, write and understand the meaning, order and relative magnitudes of fractional numbers, moving flexibly between equivalent forms.*

## Overall Description

Students read, write, say, interpret and use fractional numbers in common use. They can order numbers and understand the relevance of the order. For example, students know that one quarter of a pizza is more than one fifth of it and that cordial, which is one quarter concentrate, will be stronger than cordial, which is one fifth concentrate. However, students also know that one quarter of one pizza might be smaller than one fifth of a different-sized pizza. They understand the relative magnitudes of numbers, for example, '30% off' is not quite as good as 'one third off' and one hundredth is one tenth as big as a tenth. Students choose forms of numbers helpful in particular contexts and recognise common equivalences, such as one fifth is the same as $\frac{1}{5}$, two tenths, 0.2 and 20%. Students interpret large and small numbers for which few visual or concrete referents are available and they represent them, including with scientific notation.

| Levels of Achievement | Pointers — Progress will be evident when students: | |
|---|---|---|
| Students have achieved Level 2 when they understand the meaning of 'half' and 'quarter', splitting quantities into 'fair' shares and partitioning quantities repeatedly into halves. | • link the action of sharing into two equal portions with the language of 'half', so understand 'half' as a quantitative unit<br>• see the need to check that the 'halves' are the same size and attempt to monitor portions<br>• understand that constructing fair shares from a whole requires splitting all of the whole into equal parts (with approximate equality and exhaustion) | • attempt to produce equal shares of discrete quantities through dealing out and counting<br>• attempt to produce equal shares of continuous quantities by weighing, cutting or pouring<br>• use halving based on symmetry as basis for partitioning continuous quantities into four (eight) parts |
| Students have achieved Level 3 when they read, write, say and understand the meaning of unit fractions, flexibly partitioning and rearranging quantities to show equal parts. | • link the action of sharing into a number of equal portions with the language of unit fractions; e.g. *If I make five equal portions, then each portion is one fifth of the whole.*<br>• use fractional words (one half, third, quarter, ... tenth) appropriately in describing and comparing things; e.g. I ate about a quarter of my egg, but you ate about half.<br>• separate objects and collections into equal parts to show unit fractions; e.g. they can find one third of a cup of sugar or one fifth of the dough<br>• separate objects and collections into equal parts to compare unit fractions; e.g. they can show that half the crayons is more than a third of them | • describe and record simple fractional equivalences in words; e.g. say, *We found that the left over half pizza was as much as our two quarters put together;* and write, *One half = two quarters or 1 half = 2 quarters*<br>• 'count' orally in (common) fractional amounts; e.g. *One third, two thirds, one, one and one third*<br>• mark thirds off on a paper strip (number line); e.g. *1 third, 2 thirds, 3 thirds = 1 whole, 1 and 1 third, 1 and 2 thirds*<br>• read and write fractional notation (i.e. symbols) to represent unit fractions, e.g. $\frac{1}{3}$<br>• use basic division facts to find a unit fraction of a whole-number multiple; e.g. *There are 28 jelly beans and I will get one quarter. How many beans will I get?* |
| Students have achieved Level 4 when they read, write, say and understand the meaning of fractions and, for readily visualised fractions, estimate their relative size and position on a number line and show equivalence between them. | • use materials and diagrams to represent fractional amounts where the 'whole' may be an object, quantity or collection; e.g. they can fold tape into five equal parts and shade three parts to show $\frac{3}{5}$, or find $\frac{3}{5}$ of a collection of 20 things<br>• use equivalences that are readily visualised (i.e. pictured in the mind) to compare and order fractions; e.g. *One quarter is less than three eighths because I can 'see' that one quarter is the same as two eighths.*<br>• order fractions where the denominator changes and explain the order either in objects, diagrams or words; e.g. they can order $\frac{4}{5}$, $\frac{4}{6}$, $\frac{4}{7}$, saying that fifths are bigger than sixths which are bigger than sevenths | • estimate the position of a sequence of fractions on a number line; e.g. mark $\frac{1}{3}$, $\frac{2}{3}$, 1, 1$\frac{1}{3}$ on a paper strip marked 0, 1, 2, 3, 4<br>• use judgments of length to estimate the position of fractions on a number line; e.g. estimate to locate $\frac{4}{5}$<br>• understand that fractions are relative to particular wholes; e.g. they can explain one quarter of the family-size pizza is more than half of the small pizza<br>• share an object or collection in different ways to generate equivalent statements; e.g. three identical pizzas could be shared among four people in several 'fair' ways leading to $3 \div 4 = \frac{3}{4} = \frac{1}{4} + \frac{1}{4} + \frac{1}{4} = \frac{1}{4} + \frac{1}{2}$ |
| Students have achieved Level 5 when they read, write, say and understand the meaning, order and relative magnitude of any fractions, straightforward ratios and percentages, and know the more common equivalences between them. | • draw or visualise a diagram to compare two fractions; e.g. sketch two thirds and three quarters carefully; say, *Two thirds must be less than four fifths because if you imagine a cake, the first has a third cut out of it but the second only has a fifth cut out of it.*<br>• express two fractions with a common denominator in order to decide which is bigger; e.g. 2 fifths is smaller than 3 sevenths because the first is 14 thirty fifths and the second is 15 thirty fifths<br>• draw diagrams to represent ratios of parts to parts; e.g. they can mark a drawing of a paint can to represent the ratio of red paint to white paint as 2 to 3; or mark a picture of 30 students to represent a ratio of 2 girls to 3 boys.<br>• distinguish common fractions that show the ratio of parts to the whole from ratios which describe parts to parts; e.g. say, *The cordial to water was 1 to 4. That is, 1 part of cordial in 5 parts of drink altogether, so the fraction of cordial is one fifth.* | • use unitary ratios (i.e. of the form '1 part to b parts') when making comparisons of parts to parts; e.g. say, *In the first lot, the ratio of cordial to water was 1 to 4. That was too strong, so I added more water which made it 1 to 5.*<br>• recognise a percentage as a way of describing a ratio of part to whole, where all the denominators have been made 100 to make comparison easier<br>• interpret and use percentages to make straightforward comparisons; e.g. say, *This morning, I got 26 balls from 50 tries, that's 52%. This afternoon, I got 24 from 40 tries, that's 60%. I must be improving.*<br>• use the more common equivalences between common fractions and percentages when comparing quantities; e.g. *50% is the same as a half. One third off is better than 30% off.* |

# Key Understandings

Teachers will need to plan learning experiences that include and develop the following Key Understandings (KU), which underpin achievement of the outcome. The learning experiences should connect to students' current knowledge and understandings rather than to their year level.

| Key Understanding | Stage of Primary Schooling—Major Emphasis | KU Description | Sample Learning Activities |
|---|---|---|---|
| **KU1** When we split something into two equal-sized parts, we say we have halved it and that each part is half the original thing. | Beginning ✔✔✔<br>Middle ✔✔✔<br>Later ✔✔ | page 88 | Beginning, page 90<br>Middle, page 92<br>Later, page 95 |
| **KU2** We can partition objects and collections into two or more equal-sized parts and the partitioning can be done in different ways. | Beginning ✔✔<br>Middle ✔✔✔<br>Later ✔✔✔ | page 100 | Beginning, page 102<br>Middle, page 104<br>Later, page 106 |
| **KU3** We use fraction words and symbols to describe parts of a whole. The whole can be an object, a collection or a quantity. | Beginning ✔<br>Middle ✔✔<br>Later ✔✔✔ | page 112 | Beginning, page 114<br>Middle, page 116<br>Later, page 119 |
| **KU4** The same fractional quantity can be represented with a lot of different fractions. We say fractions are equivalent when they represent the same number or quantity. | Beginning ✔<br>Middle ✔✔<br>Later ✔✔✔ | page 122 | Beginning, page 124<br>Middle, page 125<br>Later, page 128 |
| **KU5** We can compare and order fractional numbers and place them on a number line. | Beginning ✔<br>Middle ✔✔<br>Later ✔✔ | page 130 | Beginning, page 132<br>Middle, page 133<br>Later, page 135 |
| **KU6** A fractional number can be written as a division or as a decimal. | Beginning ✔<br>Middle ✔✔<br>Later ✔✔✔ | page 140 | Beginning, page 142<br>Middle, page 143<br>Later, page 145 |
| **KU7** A fraction symbol may show a ratio relationship between two quantities. Percentages are a special kind of ratio we use to make comparisons easier. | Beginning ✔<br>Middle ✔✔<br>Later ✔✔✔ | page 148 | Beginning, page 150<br>Middle, page 151<br>Later, page 153 |

**Key**

✔✔✔ The development of this Key Understanding is a major focus of planned activities.

✔✔ The development of this Key Understanding is an important focus of planned activities.

✔ Some activities may be planned to introduce this Key Understanding, to consolidate it, or to extend its application. The idea may also arise incidentally in conversations and routines that occur in the classroom.

## KEY UNDERSTANDING 1

*When we split something into two equal-sized parts, we say we have halved it and that each part is half the original thing.*

The ideas underlying the concepts of 'halving' and a 'half' are the same as those about partitioning and fractions described in Key Understandings 2 and 3. However, half and halving are worth special attention because students often come to school with social meanings that need to be refined. Some students will associate the word 'half' with fairness and sharing. They will use it to refer to any number of shares, for example: *We all got half.* Others will associate the word 'half' with two and use it whenever there are two parts even if they are not of equal size. Halving will often simply mean to split or to share. Students' use of these words should be refined during the early primary years. Furthermore, time spent on developing and extending the notion of 'half' and learning to partition into halves (quarters and eighths) in a variety of ways assists older students to learn more general concepts about partitioning and fractions.

Students should be encouraged to use a variety of strategies, such as symmetry, dealing out, or measuring to partition quantities into two equal shares, and learn to name each equal share 'a half'. They will learn to recognise half of a half as 'a quarter' and to partition again to form eighths. For example, students might find one quarter of a pie by halving it and then halving it again. They might separate the class into four quarters by 'sharing' class members into four teams.

The idea of half should be revisited throughout the primary years so that students come to see that the equality of two 'halves' refers to the relevant quantity, not appearance. That is, two halves of something need not look alike, but they must have the same 'amount'. Objects and collections can be split into halves in many different ways. A half may be one part of two, or two parts of four, four parts of eight, five parts of ten, and so on. Also, the parts may be in any arrangement. Students should become flexible in generating different partitions and be expected to justify that their partitions do produce two equal portions.

Students who have achieved Level 2 of the outcome link the action of splitting into two equal parts with the language of 'halving'. Being able to 'colour in' half on pre-drawn and partitioned shapes is not sufficient by itself to demonstrate achievement at this level. Students must be able to produce the partition for themselves and name each part as 'one half'. These students might not yet be able to get the parts quite right, but they know the parts should be equal and will attempt to produce equal parts. However, students at this level may expect two halves to look the same and they may think there can only be two pieces.

Students who have achieved Level 3 will not be influenced by appearance and will realise, for example, that two containers may each hold half the water and yet look different. They will themselves flexibly partition and rearrange quantities in order to show that two parts are equal. For example, they can fold or cut rectangles in a variety of ways to show two halves that 'look different' but have the same area. These students recognise that one half of a quantity is one *in each two parts*, so that one half may also be thought of and named as two quarters, three sixths, four eighths, and so on.

# SAMPLE LEARNING ACTIVITIES

## Beginning ✔✔✔

### Fair Shares

Organise students into pairs, then distribute a range of materials (e.g. string, blocks, pop sticks, paper) to each pair. Ask students to share each type of material fairly with their partners. Discuss: How do you know you have fair (equal) shares? When we share into two equal portions, what do we call each portion? Is it still a half if the portions are not equal? Use the word 'half' only when referring to equal portions.

### Everyday Halves

Invite students to explain the meaning of a half in everyday situations. Examples could include half a sandwich, half an orange, half a packet of sweets, half the class. Ask students how they know it is a half in each case. Ask: What if you heard a person say, 'I want the biggest half', what could that mean?

### Halving

Have students focus on the act of halving in activities that require them to, for example: halve an apple, halve some modelling clay, halve a sheet of paper, halve their sweets. Discuss with students what they need to think about in each case. Encourage students to count or use one-to-one matching strategies to make sure the portions are equal. Have them decide what to do if an item is left over. Ask: Is that the only way you can halve it? What if a pen is left over? Will you still have half the pens if you don't share them all? Later, extend this activity by asking: What will you want to do with the half? How does that affect how you halve it? (See Sample Lesson 1, page 97.)

### Sharing Strategies

Ask students to practise halving objects and collections for a purpose. For example, say: Share this stick of celery, these pieces of carrot and a bottle of water between the two rabbits so they get half each. Have students explain why the strategies do or don't work.

### Chocolate Bars

Have students fold or cut several identical rectangular pieces of paper to represent dividing chocolate bars into halves in different ways. Ask students to find ways to check that each 'chocolate bar' is in halves.

### Half a Dozen

Ask students to use an egg carton and eggs to show how six white eggs and six brown eggs could each be half a dozen. Ask students to represent this in a diagram. Then, have students draw another arrangement and ask: Are half of the eggs still brown? What would have to change so that half of the eggs are not white?

### Half Measures

Invite students to use a half-cup measure to make recipes given in whole-cup measures. Have them discuss and predict how many half-cup measures will be needed for various numbers of whole cups and then arrive at a rule. Test students' predictions using sand and whole- and half-cup measures.

### Function Box

Place different objects and collections inside a large cardboard box (Halving Machine). Then, have one or more students inside the box halve whatever is put inside the machine. For example, six marbles become three marbles. Ask the other students to check the accuracy of the machine, justifying their conclusions each time. (See also Reason About Number Patterns, Key Understanding 3.)

### Approximate/Exact

Ask students to identify and list situations in which the word 'half' is used. Then, have students distinguish between the casual, everyday use of 'half' as an approximation, and when the use of 'half' is intended to convey an exact quantity. For example, half an apple might not be exact whereas half of ten jelly beans will be.

## SAMPLE LEARNING ACTIVITIES

# Middle ✔✔✔

### Partitioning Paper

Have students find ways to partition a strip of paper into two equal lengths and explain why each part is called a half. Students then halve the halves and, looking at the whole strip, name the four equal parts, saying why they are quarters. Repeat this activity for eighths. After several partitions, invite students to say what is happening to the number of parts. Ask: What is happening to the length of each part?

### Collections

Extend the 'Partitioning Paper' activity using different collections (e.g. counters). Have students investigate the effects of repeatedly halving the collection. Invite them to explore why some collections can be repeatedly halved until one item remains, while some cannot be halved at all, assuming a single counter cannot be halved. (Link to Understand Operations, Key Understanding 5.)

### Comparing Halves

Ask students to take two strips of paper of different lengths and colours, then halve each strip. Have them compare the halves and discuss: If halves have to be equal, why aren't these halves the same length?

### Halving Grids

Have students colour half the squares on 4 x 4 grids to show different representations of a half. Invite them to discuss what must be checked in each case to be sure half is coloured. Then, ask students to draw diagonal lines across the squares in a grid, making each square into two triangles. Ask: What new ways can you find to colour half of the grid?

### Sorting Shapes

Ask students to sort shapes according to whether they have half the area shaded or not. Have students cut out and rearrange the parts to decide. For example:

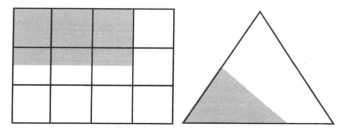

**Not equal to half**

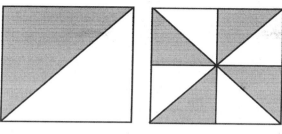

**Equal to half**

This activity can be linked to situations where students are asked to decide whether two different shapes have the same area. (Link also to Direct Measure, Key Understanding 2.)

**Comparing Fractions**

Have students cut and rearrange parts of shapes to compare fractions that look different. Ask: Can these both be quarters? What new ways of shading a quarter of the square could we make?

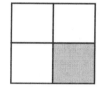 

Repeat this activity using circles and triangles, and halves and eighths. (Link to Direct Measure, Key Understanding 2.)

**Half?**

Show students a piece of paper marked to show two portions as shown below. Invite students to use paper tiles and grid paper to decide whether the paper has been divided into halves.

**Measuring Half**

Ask students to use ways other than counting to separate a quantity of paperclips into halves. Students could use balance scales (mass), spread out the paperclips on grid paper (area), link the paperclips in a chain and then halve (length), or they could pour the paperclips into two identical tumblers (volume). Have students count to check the equality of the halves, then discuss the relative accuracy and time it took to find the halves using each method. (Link to Direct Measure, Key Understanding 1.)

# Middle ✔✔✔

### Halving Wholes

Have students find different ways to halve a range of wholes. For example, half a ribbon could be half the length of the ribbon, or half the width of the ribbon. Or, a student might say: *I cut the ribbon into eight equal pieces. Half is four of these pieces.* Invite students to discuss how the halves are the same or different.

### Chocolate Bars

Extend the Beginning Sample Learning Activity, 'Chocolate Bars', by asking students to select two halves (pieces of paper) that look different. Ask: If these were two different halves of chocolate bars, would two people each get the same amount of chocolate to eat? If you gave one person this half of a chocolate bar: ▣▢ , and another person this half of a chocolate bar: ▭ , would they get the same amount to eat? How do you know?

# SAMPLE LEARNING ACTIVITIES

## Later ✔✔

### Half Recipes

Ask students to rewrite cake recipes as 'half recipes'. Discuss issues such as: Do we bake the cake for half the time? If the recipe says, 'use a 20-centimetre cake tin', how do I choose one that is 'half' as big?

### Halves, Quarters, Eighths

Have students fold a paper circle in half, then draw around one half and label it ' $\frac{1}{2}$ '. Ask them to fold the circle in half again, then draw around one quarter and label it ' $\frac{1}{4}$ '. Then, have students fold the paper again, draw around one eighth and label it ' $\frac{1}{8}$ '. Ask students to continue until the 'slice' is too small to fold and label. Invite students to continue the pattern using numbers alone. Ask: How can you prove that the fraction named is correct? (Link to Reason About Number Patterns, Key Understandings 2, 3 and 4.)

### Halving Patterns

Invite students to use a long strip of paper to explore halving and re-halving, naming the new fractional parts each time. Ask them to try to extend the pattern in order to answer questions such as: What would you have after halving the paper five times? What about after ten times? Give students several very large denominators and challenge them to show if these could be in the 'halving pattern' or not. (Link to Reason About Number Patterns, Key Understandings 2, 3 and 4.)

### Halving Unit Fractions

Have students use strips of paper to investigate finding a half of different unit fractions. First, students fold the strip into thirds, then they fold the strip in half and say what they did. For example, *I folded my thirds in half and got sixths*. Invite students to try to find a rule for halving any unit fraction. Ask: Does the rule also work for other fractions, such as $\frac{3}{4}$ or $\frac{4}{5}$?

### Finding Half

Provide students with a range of 4 x 4 grids that have been partly shaded (include squares divided diagonally into two and four triangles). Ask students to identify the shapes in which exactly half the area has been shaded. Have them justify their choices. Then, ask students to use blank 4 x 4 grids to find other ways to shade half the area.

# Later ✔✔

### Cows in a Paddock

Show students different-shaped pieces of paper, each marked to show two portions like the illustrations below. Say: A farmer has divided his paddocks like this. Will the cows in each part of each paddock get the same amount of grass?

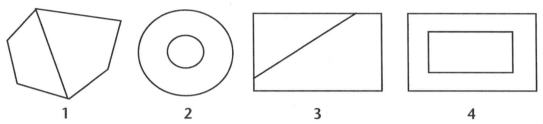

Then, invite students to cut out and rearrange the pieces of paper to prove or disprove that the portions are equal in area. Extend this activity to ask students to draw paddocks with two parts, which look different, but which students can show must be half each. (Link to Direct Measure, Key Understanding 2.)

### Half Sayings

Have students list situations in which 'half' is used colloquially to refer to attributes not usually measured. For example: *Half your time has been wasted looking out the window; I wish I was half as good at basketball as you are.* Discuss with students mathematical ways they could test the truth of such statements.

### Representing Half

Ask each student to make a 'Half' book to give to a Year 1 or Year 2 student. Discuss the important aspects that should be included and all the different ways that a half might be represented. Students might include representations where the two halves look distinctly different, and write: *Can you say why these are halves?* They might also include representations of two shares that are not halves, and write: *These are not halves. Can you say why?*

### Sharing Halves

Have students explore unusual ways of sharing different items into halves. Ask them to explain the context in which their halving might make sense. For example: *A cake is cut into appropriate-sized pieces. There are seven pieces to share between two people. They share the pieces, then cut the leftover piece in half. So, half of the cake is three sevenths and one fourteenth of the cake.* (Link to Key Understanding 6, Later Sample Learning Activity, 'More Sharing'.)

## SAMPLE LESSON 1

**Sample Learning Activity:** Beginning—'Halving', page 90

**Key Understanding 1:** When we split something into two equal-sized parts, we say we have halved it and that each part is half the original thing.

**Working Towards:** Levels 2 and 3

### Teacher's Purpose

I knew my Year 3 students had a notion of 'half' as 'one of two parts'. However, I was not confident they understood that for the two portions or parts to be halves they must have the same quantity or size. I decided to provide some learning experiences that would help my students develop the idea of equal portions.

### Connection and Challenge

I helped my students make Fairy Bread (slices of bread and butter sprinkled with 'Hundreds and Thousands') for a parents' morning tea. I asked them to cut each slice in half and then half again. Most students cut the bread into four rectangles or four triangles and attempted to make the portions roughly equal. However, I was not sure whether this was due to their idea of sharing food rather than their knowing what 'half' means.

A few days later, I organised students into pairs and gave each student a square piece of paper. I asked them to find as many different ways as they could to give their partner exactly half of a slice of 'Fairy Bread'. Most students began with standard cuts:

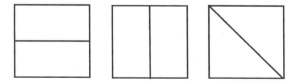

As my students tried to find other alternatives, they began to expose their ideas about halves. They focused on physically varying the two portions and showed little concern for making the portions equal. Some students thought any two pieces could be halves. Others cut their square into four pieces and gave their partner two pieces. We often cut bread into four pieces, so this made sense to the students in the context of bread. They were not concerned about making the pieces the same size.

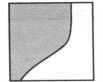 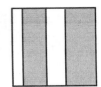    

**The shaded sections show one person's share.**

Jamie looked confused when I asked how he could be sure the two portions he had made were halves. His partner, Erica, spoke for him, 'There are two pieces. One for him and one for me.'

'But one piece is a lot smaller than the other,' I said.

'Well,' said Erica, 'If it was really Fairy Bread, you would cut it in the middle, so that would be fair. But, we cut one piece in the middle and now we're doing a different one.'

'Have you still cut it in halves though? Can you still call it a half if it's bigger than the other piece?' I asked.

Erica hesitated, but Jamie didn't, 'That's the big half and Erica got the little half.'

## Drawing Out the Mathematical Idea

Having heard similar comments from other students, I brought the whole class together to establish the idea of equality as an essential element of halving. I asked pairs of students to show some of their halves to the class and invited the rest of the class to comment. This gave the few students who did know about the need for equality an opportunity to question some of the unequal partitions.

In the end, it was Alisha who insisted the halves had to be the same size. Alisha demonstrated this by putting pieces on top of each other to prove her partitions were halves. Then, she explained that if the pieces did not match, they could not be halves. While I knew that this was an oversimplification and that the halves do not have to fit over each other exactly, I let it pass for now. Instead, I choose to draw out the idea that to be called 'halves' the parts have to have the same amount, 'You and your partner have to get exactly the same amount of Fairy Bread to eat. Otherwise, you can't say you have cut the bread in half.'

*Students cannot 'discover' that fractional parts have to be equal from activities with materials since it is not an 'empirical' fact. Rather, it is what people mean by the word. Some students will infer the correct meaning from how the term is used in everyday contexts but, generally, it will help to make this explicit.*

The students then went through their shares, matching the pieces as Alisha had. They separated those pieces that looked like halves from those that did not.

Later, I set out a selection of materials, including paper plates, string, cotton wool balls, rice, beans, popsicle sticks, straws, modelling clay, half a glass of coloured water, a sheet of paper, jelly beans, mints, counters, blocks, paper tape and matchsticks. Each pair of students took various quantities of five different types of materials.

Emphasising that each half must have an 'equal amount', I asked students to give their partner half of each type of material. They then had to draw the two halves and write what they did on a chart, so that someone looking at it could see they really had halved the materials.

After they had been working for a short while, I asked different students to explain what they'd done and how they knew for sure they'd shared the material into halves. I thought from their responses that the need for equality of the two parts had connected. For example, Tanya folded the string in half and cut it into two. I asked, 'How do you know this piece is really a half?'

Tanya picked up one piece and laid it carefully next to the other. Seeing that one piece was actually a little longer than the other, she said, 'Oh, it's not half. I folded the string in half like this, but I must have cut it wrong.' Tanya knew that because the pieces of string were unequal in length, they could not be called halves.

I asked Tanya, 'How could you fix it so it really is in halves?'

Tanya used her scissors to cut off the extra piece and said triumphantly, 'Now, it's halves. They're the same size.'

Tanya's response made me realise that by focusing the students' attention on equality of parts, the importance of the whole had been de-emphasised. After calling for help from nearby students, we established that although the pieces were now the same length, not all of the string was there. You couldn't say that each piece was half of the original length of string. Tanya then realised she could cut the extra piece into two equal pieces so each half had a long piece and a tiny piece.

* straws
* cotton wool
* rice
* beans
* jelly beans
* counters

## Reflecting on Learning

The students' charts were displayed and became a topic of discussion over the following weeks. This consolidated their understanding and provided them with opportunities to practise the language while comparing their work. For example, three paper plates were halved in two distinctly different ways:

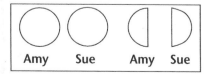
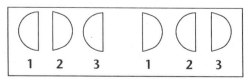

I noted that most of the students seemed to believe that to be halves, the two parts had to look identical. Working towards overcoming this mistaken idea would be the focus of future activities.

## KEY UNDERSTANDING 2

*We can partition objects and collections into two or more equal-sized parts and the partitioning can be done in different ways.*

The idea that things can be partitioned or split into parts of equal size underpins the fraction concept. Partitioning into halves is dealt with in Key Understanding 1, but partitioning into any number of parts is dealt with here. Key Understanding 2 is also a key to the development of Understand Operations (Key Understanding 5) and Calculate (Key Understanding 3), underlining its significance in linking multiplication, division and fractions.

Students need extensive experience in splitting a diverse range of discrete and continuous wholes into equal-sized parts. Collections (discrete quantities) can be shared into equal parts by dealing out or distributing, while objects can be shared into equal parts by cutting, folding, drawing, pouring and weighing. Students should become flexible in partitioning and develop the following ideas.

- Equal parts need not look alike, but they must have the same size or amount of the relevant quantity.

- When splitting a whole into equal parts, the whole should be completely used up.

- Regardless of how we partition, the whole remains the same amount.

- The more shares something is split into, the smaller each share is.

These ideas are not straightforward. For example, students will often think that 'equal parts' means that the parts have to look alike. In reality, the parts may look different, but still be equal in size. So, if we halve a lump of modelling clay by mass and use each piece to produce different-looking objects, there are still equal quantities of modelling clay. Also, young students may neglect to use up the entire whole, discarding remaining portions rather than distributing them into the equal groups.

Students need to be able to construct a suitable partition without being given a pre-drawn diagram. They should, for example, be able to construct their own partition into four parts, then partition an identical thing into six parts, and then consider how many partitions would be needed to enable them to show four equal parts as well as six equal parts. This supports the notion of finding common denominators, which is the basis for finding equivalent fractions, comparing and ordering fractions and for calculating with them (see Calculate, Key Understanding 7).

Students who have achieved Level 3 of the outcome have generalised their knowledge of partitioning into two parts to the idea of partitioning into two, three, four, five or more equal groups in straightforward situations. Students are not concerned by appearance. They accept that the parts could look different, but still be equal in size. These students are becoming more careful in their partitioning, but their geometric or measurement knowledge may not be sufficient to enable them to consistently produce correct partitions.

At Level 4, students have increased the flexibility of their partitioning and are able to partition an object or collection to show, for example, four equal parts and six equal parts. With prompting, students can try to do this in the fewest number of parts. Those students who have achieved Level 5 will autonomously apply this skill to drawing and visualising diagrams to compare two fractions with unlike denominators and to adding and subtracting fractions. (Link to Calculate, Key Understanding 7.)

## SAMPLE LEARNING ACTIVITIES

### Beginning ✔✔

**Fair Shares**

Ask: What is a 'fair share'? Can you give me some examples? Discuss everyday examples, such as: family meals, where a 'fair share' may reflect age and food needs; the amount of pocket money paid for jobs done around the house; sharing sweets into equal numbers; sharing pieces of fruit into equal quantities. Brainstorm sharing situations where equality of quantity is important.

**Segments**

Ask students to peel and segment a piece of citrus fruit, such as a mandarin, and decide if the segments are equal in size. If the segments are equal, then invite students to explain how three (five, six, seven, eight) people could share the whole mandarin.

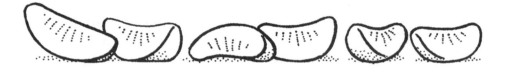

**Making a Sandwich**

Have students cut a 'sandwich' (square piece of paper) into four equal parts. Once students have done this, ask: Can you think of another way to cut the sandwich into four equal parts? Ask students to prove that the pieces are the same size by superimposing, or by cutting and rearranging, to cover the same area. (See also 'Did You Know?', page 127.)

**Sharing Collections**

Have students share collections that can be easily subdivided. For example, 12 slices of Fairy Bread between two (three, four) plates, so that each plate has the same amount of Fairy Bread. Then, have students try five plates. Ask: Why is it difficult to share 12 slices between five plates? When is sharing collections easy? When is it difficult?

### Equal Shares

Read to the class familiar stories, such as *The Doorbell Rang* by Pat Hutchins. Then, ask students to say how many equal shares the collection is subdivided into each time. Ask: Why would it be difficult to share 24 between five people? When is making equal portions easy? When is it difficult? (Link to Understand Operations, Key Understanding 4.)

### Equal Pieces

Invite students to explore different ways of breaking a liquorice strap into three equal pieces. Encourage students to experiment with strips of paper before actually cutting the liquorice. Ask students to explain how they made sure that all pieces were the same amount and that all liquorice was used. Repeat this activity for five pieces.

### Sharing Equally

Organise students into groups of four. Give each group a lump of modelling clay. Ask students to share the modelling clay equally. Discuss with students how they can be sure that the shares are equal. Ask: What fraction of the modelling clay have you got? Have each of you really got a quarter of the modelling clay? Invite students to think of different ways of checking the equivalence of the four pieces.

### Thirds

Organise students into groups of three. Give each group a jug of water and a number of clear plastic drink containers. Ask students to share the water among themselves, making sure they each get a third.

### Party Baskets

Have students investigate ways of sharing different numbers of sweets among different numbers of party baskets without leftovers or cutting up the sweets. Ask students to make a class chart that shows how many sweets they could buy to share equally between different numbers of baskets.

### Grouping

Give students collections of discrete items that cannot be cut up (e.g. blocks, shells). Then, ask them to sort the items into two groups: those that can be shared into equal groups and those that cannot. Have students record the numbers and discuss results. Ask: Which collections can be halved and which collections cannot? Introduce the terms 'even' and 'odd' numbers to describe the two categories. Ask: Can you find a third of your collection? Why? Why not? (Link to Understand Operations, Key Understanding 5.)

# SAMPLE LEARNING ACTIVITIES

## Middle ✔✔✔

### Sharing a Pizza

Have students cut up a variety of different-sized paper circle 'pizzas' into different numbers of equal shares. Explore questions, such as: If each of us eats three slices of our pizzas, and our pizzas are the same size, how could you eat more than me? If we each eat one third of our pizzas, how could I eat more slices than you?

### Three Colours

Ask students to use three colours to shade a 3 x 3 square grid, making sure that each colour covers an equal area of the grid. Then, invite students to explore the number of different ways they can make thirds using the same three colours. Have students explain how they know each arrangement has equal amounts of each colour and is showing thirds. Repeat this activity for other grids to shade five (six, seven, eight) equal parts and link this to the appropriate fractions.

### Equal Portions

Have students use materials (e.g. counters) to decide how many different ways a packet of 24 sweets could be split into equal portions. Ask students to record these on a class chart. For example, 24 can be split into two, three, four, six, eight, 12 and 24 equal portions. (Link to Understand Operations, Key Understanding 5.)

### Equal Groupings

Vary the 'Equal Portions' activity. Ask students to draw diagrams to decide on the number of equal groupings in different-sized collections of, for example, seven (11, 12, 13, 21, 29) objects.

### Chocolate Bars

Have students use diagrams to decide how to share any number of chocolate bars between three people. For example, students describe, cut and rearrange, or shade one or more bars to work out how to partition all of the chocolate into three equal portions. Ask: How many ways could the chocolate bars be divided to give equal portions? (See Key Understanding 1.)

**KU 2**

### Orange Juice

Ask students to investigate the results of sharing a container of orange juice holding five cupfuls. Ask: If there is less than five people, what do we know about how much each person will get? What if there were more than five people? How could we describe the shares?

### Sharing Large Collections

Invite students to use a range of methods to share large collections into equal parts. For example, say: I have one bag of macaroni and I plan to eat an equal amount of it each night over the next five days. Have students use different methods to make five equal portions.

### Pets

Ask students to share different types of materials into the same number of equal parts. For example, say: Share food and water equally between a number of pets. Discuss strategies for ensuring equality of parts when all of the whole must be used up. (See Sample Lesson 2, page 109.)

### Pattern Blocks

Have students use geometrically designed materials, such as pattern blocks, to partition the larger shapes into equal parts. For example, ask: How many different equal parts can a hexagon be partitioned into?

### Multiple Slices

Invite students to investigate different sharing contexts using materials (e.g. paper plates) or diagrams to partition things so that they can be shared equally by groups of different sizes. For example, say: Grandad likes to slice the pizza so that it can be shared equally by the grandchildren, but he isn't always sure how many grandchildren will come. How will Grandad need to slice the pizza if two or four grandchildren come to his house? What about for two or six (two, four or eight) grandchildren? What is the smallest number of slices Grandad needs to make in each case? Repeat for other examples where one number is a factor of the other. Ask: What is it about these numbers of grandchildren that makes it easy to work out how many slices you need to make? (Link to Calculate, Key Understanding 3.)

### Sharing with Odd Numbers

Repeat the 'Multiple Slices' activity to include numbers that do not have a common factor. Ask: How would Grandad need to slice the pizza if he wasn't sure whether two or three grandchildren were coming? What about if four or five grandchildren were coming? Draw out the idea that the number of slices has to be a multiple of each number of grandchildren. (See also 'Sharing Sweets', Middle Sample Learning Activities, in Understand Operations, Key Understanding 5.)

## SAMPLE LEARNING ACTIVITIES

### Later ✔✔✔

**Patterns**

Organise students into pairs. Then, ask each student to design tile patterns using equal quantities of three colours on grids. For example:

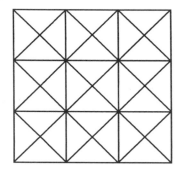

Ask students to give their designs to a partner to check that one third is covered by each colour.

**Rations**

Ask students to partition a range of materials (e.g. blocks, counters) or create diagrams in order to decide how much each person would receive in a given situation. For example, say: You are one of ten people stranded in a forest. You must share the food, which includes one loaf of sliced bread, seven apples, four litres of water and 25 sausages. Describe each person's share. Discuss: How did you share the rations? (Link to Understand Operations, Key Understanding 5, and Calculate, Key Understanding 10.)

**Rectangles**

Have students make a list of rectangles that can be made from a specified number of tiles. For example, with 16 tiles, students can make rectangles with one, two, four, eight or 16 rows of tiles. Have students look for fractions within their rectangles and draw diagrams to illustrate; for example:

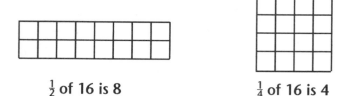

$\frac{1}{2}$ of 16 is 8          $\frac{1}{4}$ of 16 is 4

Repeat for other numbers. Build up a class table for collections from 1 to 100. Later, use it to identify factors as well as odd, even, composite and prime numbers. (Link to Reason About Number Patterns, Key Understanding 6.)

### Splitting a Circle

Ask students to use a protractor to split a circle into equal parts, then use the divisions for an art activity based on drawing a windmill, flower or wheel. Have students decide what fraction of the circle is needed for each vane, petal or spoke and find a way to demonstrate this.

### Fraction Sequence

Have students use a protractor or a circular grid (i.e. a printed circle divided into 36 sectors) to divide a circle into thirds, then one third into thirds. Ask students to label one third, then one ninth. Challenge them to find a third of the ninth and label it. Ask: What is the next fraction in the sequence? (Link to Reason About Number Patterns, Key Understanding 2.)

### Dividing Land

Provide students with 10 x 10 grids to represent a farmer's block of land. Have students find different ways to divide the land into five paddocks of equal area. Ask, how can you convince the farmer that each paddock is exactly a fifth of the land area?

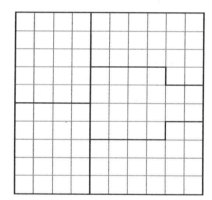 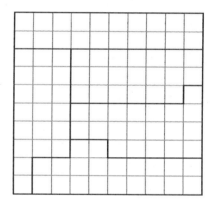

### Rules for Sharing

Invite students to explore different ways of cutting up three pies to share equally among a family of five, using paper circles to represent the pies. Then, ask students to add to a class table, beginning with one pie shared among five people, working through to at least ten pies. Try to devise a sharing 'rule' that would work no matter how many pies are to be shared. (Link to Reason About Number Patterns, Key Understandings 2 and 3.)

### Multiple Slices

Have students decide how many parts they need to partition things into so that they can be shared equally by groups of different sizes. Ask: How would Grandad need to slice the pizza if he wasn't sure whether two, four or eight grandchildren were coming? What would happen if three or five grandchildren were coming? What is different about the two situations? (Link to 'Multiple Slices', Middle Sample Learning Activities, and Understand Operations, Key Understanding 5.)

# Later ✔✔✔

**Common Factors**

Extend the 'Multiple Slices' activity by having students work out the number of portions needed for different groups of grandchildren that have a common factor where one number is not a factor of the other. For example, say: When Grandad thought that there could be either four or six grandchildren coming, he said, 'Six fours are 24.' He thought he would have to cut the pizza into 24 slices. That would be a mess. Can he cut a smaller number of slices and still be able to share the pizza equally? Try other possibilities where the number of children has a common factor and you want to get the smallest number of slices. (See also 'Equal Portions', Middle Sample Learning Activities, and Understand Operations, Key Understanding 5.)

## *Did You Know?*

**A diagnostic activity for the middle and later years**

Pose the following problem.

**Kia and Sam had different types of sandwiches. They decided to give each other exactly half a sandwich. The picture below shows how they cut their sandwiches into two pieces.**

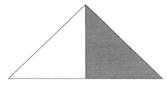

Kia's sandwich

Sam's sandwich

**Sam took the shaded part of Kia's sandwich, but Kia wasn't sure that she could take exactly half of Sam's. What should she do?**

Ask: Do you think that the shaded piece of Sam's sandwich could be a half? If you think it is possible, can you think of a way to check?

Many students initially think that halves have to match exactly; that is, look the same. Many students would not accept that the shaded shapes could be half the area of the triangle. Others—usually younger students—may think that any two parts is half and so would not bother to check at all.

## SAMPLE LESSON 2

**Sample Learning Activity:** Middle—'Pets', page 105

**Key Understanding 2:** We can partition objects and collections into two or more equal-sized parts and the partitioning can be done in different ways.

**Focus:** To be able to partition and rearrange quantities flexibly to show equal parts. We have special words and symbols for parts of a whole, where the whole can be an object, a collection or a quantity.

**Working Towards:** Levels 2 and 3

### Purpose

I organised my Year 4 students into groups. Then, I read out loud the following problem and showed the students the materials mentioned in the activity.

*My friend has three rabbits that she keeps in three different cages. She has some things to be shared between the rabbits. There is a bag of sand for the bottom of their cages, a bottle of water for them to share, some carrots and a long stick of celery to eat. Show how my friend could share these things fairly between the rabbits so each one gets a third of the supplies.*

Each group was told that they needed to discuss the problem, then agree on the methods for sharing each type of material, before carrying out their plans.

### Action and Reflection

As the students discussed their strategies, I moved among the groups listening to their ideas. However, I did not intervene or make any suggestions. For the carrots and the sand, most students used dealing-out strategies; for example: one cup of sand for that rabbit, one for this rabbit and one for the other rabbit. They continued to do this until there wasn't any more sand. For the other materials, students looked for ways to physically partition into three and adjust quantities by matching.

'We can get three science beakers and pour the water in them until they all line up,' suggested Sian.

'We could cut paper tape for the celery, fold it in three and then cut along the folds,' said Marino.

*At a workshop, a teacher said many of her students thought fractions were shapes. The group thought this may have been because students were often only given activities in which they coloured in parts of shapes that have already been divided up. Thus, these students associate fractions with colouring and counting parts of shapes. As a result, I decided to get my students to partition a range of wholes.*

I asked various groups to explain how they were certain the resulting shares were equal. Those students who were partitioning by physically comparing the three parts—for example, the height of the water in the three beakers, or the lengths of the three sections of celery—seemed to have little difficulty. However, the students sharing by dealing out found it more difficult.

What to do with the leftovers became an issue. The students' solutions revealed a lot more about their current ideas on equal sharing. A number of students seemed to think they should dispose of the excess in some way so that the shares remained equal. Andrew ate the one leftover piece of carrot saying, 'That makes the shares the same.'

While there were objections about this from the rest of the group ('We're not supposed to eat it ourselves!'), no one said that all the carrot pieces had to be shared out.

Other students wanted to make sure they used up all of the materials, but they were less bothered about ensuring equality. Jason was half a cup of sand short in the last round and said, 'It doesn't really matter. We used all the sand and it's only a bit less in one. It's not going to make any difference to the rabbits!'

The rest of Jason's group was quite happy to go along with this suggestion.

## Drawing Out the Mathematical Idea

I stopped the class and asked the students to think about whether their sharing of the sand fitted the two criteria of 'equal parts' and 'using up all the supplies'. We talked about the difference between unequal sharing, or only using part of the whole, as a way of dealing with everyday situations. We also discussed what it means to have equal shares in mathematics.

I asked everyone to look at the partitions they'd made so far and to decide if each rabbit really did get a third of the supplies. If they were unsure, the students had to find a way to check the equality of the partitions, and to include any disposed of 'excess' materials in the final shares. I continued to ask individual students to explain in their own words what was needed to ensure each rabbit got a third of the supplies. I wanted all my students to get this important idea from the activity at a conscious level.

I noticed they began to use strategies that ensured both equality and no leftovers.

Catherine reported that her group began using a cup to share out the sand. 'We just kind of dealt it out in rounds: one for each rabbit. We got to four cups each, then there wasn't enough to do another round, so then we used

*While physical experiences of sharing in various contexts are essential for developing students' understanding of fractions, it is also essential that the meaning and language of fractions be made an explicit part of those experiences. Otherwise, students may not make the necessary mental links between the two.*

teaspoons for the rest of it. We used it all up. There are four cups and seven teaspoons of sand in each cage.'

I saw that Alphonse had two pieces of carrot left over, which his group had previously discarded. He cut both pieces in half, gave a half to each rabbit, then cut the last half into three parts (see below). I asked Alphonse why he cut the final piece of carrot like that and not a different way. I offered the second diagram as a possibility.

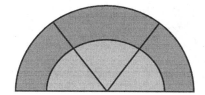

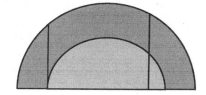

**Alphonse's diagram**          **My diagram**

Alphonse's explanation told me he was developing a good understanding of equality. He said, 'If you cut like that, you can't tell if they are really thirds. The way I cut it, it has to be thirds because they're all the same.'

Alphonse had piled the three pieces on top of one another to prove his point. His comment that a partition like mine could be thirds indicated that he knew equal amounts do not have to be the same shape. However, in this case, Alphonse chose to make them the same shape as a way of proving equality of the parts. I asked him to explain his reasoning to several other students to help them understand this other important idea about equality in maths.

## Opportunity to Learn

I was surprised that no one chose to count the twenty or so pieces of carrot and divide them by three; even though we'd been practising such calculations just the previous day. I tried to prompt one group to try this, but they seemed not to be able to see how this could work. The students did not appear to understand how partitioning into three shares to find a third of a number of items was connected to dividing a number by three. I realised I needed to plan activities that would help them see the relationships between sharing, the division operation and fractions (i.e. Key Understanding 6). I also needed to let them hear the kind of language that would help them to make the links.

## KEY UNDERSTANDING 3

*We use fraction words and symbols to describe parts of a whole. The whole can be an object, a collection or a quantity.*

Students should develop a good grasp of the vocabulary and notation of fractions. During the beginning- and middle-primary years, the emphasis should be on the meaning of fraction words rather than the symbolic form.

The most common use of fractions relates to the part-whole idea. Initially, students should learn to link the action of sharing into a number of equal portions with the language of unit fractions (that is, **one** half, **one** third, and so on). They should be able to say, for example, that there are six equal parts and so each part is 'one sixth'. Students should: find one sixth of a pie by separating it into six equal-sized parts and taking one part; fill one sixth of a jug with water; and separate the class into six equal groups, saying that the number in each group is one sixth of the number in the class. Through such activities, students should be able to demonstrate to themselves relationships, such as a quarter of a pie (jug of water or class) is more than a sixth of it. Gradually, they will develop the more complete idea that one sixth of a whole is one in **each** six parts of the whole. This understanding is necessary for understanding equivalent fractions.

Students should learn to count forwards in simple fractional amounts, relating the 'count' to actual quantities. For example, they could cut a number of identical 'cakes' into thirds and then 'count' as they pull portions to the side. That is, one third (of a cake), two thirds (of a cake), three thirds (which is one whole cake), one and a third, one and two thirds, and so on. In doing so, students should come to think, for example, of four thirds as the same as one and one third. Only after they are comfortable with the fraction words should students be expected to learn to use the symbolic conventions for reading and writing fractional amounts.

For example, if we partition something into five equal parts:

- each part is called 'one fifth' and it is written symbolically as '$\frac{1}{5}$'

- four of the parts are called 'four fifths' and are written symbolically as '$\frac{4}{5}$'.

Students should understand that to find three quarters of 'a whole', one must separate the whole into equal parts and take three out of **each** four parts. The equal parts need not look alike, but they must have the same measure of, for example: mass, length, angle or number. The whole could be an object (a banana), a collection (a bag of shells) or a quantity (the length of a trip or weight of flour). It may be a single thing, many things or a part of a thing. Sometimes, students develop the mistaken view that the 'whole' must be a single thing. They may also believe that the denominator must match the number of partitions of the whole. That is, to find three quarters the whole must be broken into only four equal parts of which three are taken. Such students may have difficulty in seeing why $\frac{3}{4} = \frac{9}{12}$. They need to think of three quarters of a collection, object or quantity as three in **each** four parts.

Students who have achieved the outcome at Level 2 use 'half' and 'halve' appropriately in context. Those students who have achieved Level 3 link the action of sharing into equal portions and taking one of the portions with the language of unit fractions (e.g. *one half, one third, one quarter, one fifth, one sixth, ... one tenth*). They use fractional words orally and in writing to describe and compare things (e.g. *I have about a third left but she only has a quarter*). They also count forwards and backwards using fractional words (e.g. *one third, two thirds, three thirds or one, one and one third*). They can also use fractional notation ($\frac{1}{5}$) for unit fractions. Students who have achieved Level 4 can use fractional words and notation fluently for the range of common fractions ($\frac{4}{5}$, $\frac{19}{5}$ or $3\frac{4}{5}$).

KU 3

## SAMPLE LEARNING ACTIVITIES

# Beginning ✔

### Fractional Language

Introduce and use fractional language incidentally during construction and play to describe how much is left or has been used. For example, say: There are about one and a half boxes of sultanas left. Find a block that is half of this one. You will need one and a half circles. The truck has about a quarter of a load. Cut off three quarters of a piece of string.

### Equal Shares

Organise students into groups. Ask them to distribute materials (e.g. rice, modelling clay, a strip of paper) within their groups in equal shares and name them using fractional language. For example: *A third of our modelling clay for Adrian, a third for Rana, and a third for me.* Encourage students to refer to the whole. For example, ask: You said you have a 'third', what is it a third of? Have students distribute materials in response to fractions requiring 'action'. For example, say: Take a quarter of the modelling clay each. Give each person in your group a quarter of the rice. Cut off half of the paper strip. Encourage students to explain how they know they have found the relevant fraction of the material used.

### One Third

Ask students to model one third in many different contexts. Have students make a 'Third' book or classroom display featuring a wide range of materials that show if any whole is split into three equal parts, each part is called 'one third'. Ask students to label each part with the word 'third' and the numeral '$\frac{1}{3}$'. Invite students to write the stories in words and draw pictures to illustrate how the shares are made equal.

### Giant's Jump

Discuss with students how big a giant's jump might be. Use chalk to mark the length of this jump on the playground. Then, have students judge how far they can jump in relation to the 'giant's jump'. Discuss with students how they can compare one of their jumps to the giant's jump and introduce fractional language to assist. For example, say: Karoly jumped about half as far as the giant. Jason jumped about a third of the giant's jump.

### Half Full

Use fractional language incidentally when describing how much is left or has been used. For example, say: You seem to have three quarters of your glue left. That's about a quarter more than Alice. Her container of glue is half full. The truck has about a quarter of a load. Cut off three quarters of this piece of string.

### Half/Quarter

Use the fractional language of 'half' and 'quarter' regularly in conjunction with whole numbers. For example, say: I have two and a half apples left. You are more than five and a half years old, so you are nearly six. Are you six and a half yet?

KU **3**

# SAMPLE LEARNING ACTIVITIES

## Middle ✔✔

### What Is the Whole?

Present students with problems where they must identify the whole when given a fractional part. For example, say: Here is one third of this chocolate bar. Draw the whole chocolate bar.

### Finding Fractions

Organise students into pairs. Then, give each pair a range of 'wholes', such as three straws, a semicircle, one cup of water, a piece of string and a bag of rice. Ask students to find a given unit fraction, such as a quarter or a third, of each of their wholes. Invite them to record, in pictures and words, how they did this and the result for each. Later, discuss with the class what is the same and what is different about each fractional amount.

### Equal Groups

Invite students to partition a box of paperclips, sweets or other discrete quantities into equal groups. For each group size, ask students to name the unit fraction represented by one group. Draw students' attention to the role of the denominator. Ask: How many parts have you got? So, what do you call one of those parts? Draw out the idea that if there are six equal parts, for example, then one of the parts is one sixth. (See 'Pets' Middle Sample Learning Activity, page 105, and Sample Lesson 2, page 109.)

### Fractional Language

Encourage students to use fractional language in response to everyday questions. For example, ask: How far did you run around the oval? What fraction of the strip of paper did you use? What fraction of the sweets do you have? How could we check that this really is about three quarters of the string?

### Measuring Metres

Organise students into groups of three. Ask the members of each group to take a metre-long strip of paper each and fold it in halves, then quarters. Have them mark the fractions on the fold lines in pencil, then join their lengths together to form a three-metre-long tape. Ask students to record in different colours the half metres and the quarter metres in sequence along the tape. Invite them to use the tape to record lengths in metres and fractions of a metre.

**Thirds**

Later, extend the 'Fractional Language' activity, so that students fold their three-metre-long tape into thirds. Then, ask them to mark thirds along the tape in different colours to halves and quarters they have already recorded ($\frac{1}{3}$, $\frac{2}{3}$, 1, 1$\frac{1}{3}$, 1$\frac{2}{3}$, 2).

**Fractions and Shapes**

Ask students to use pattern blocks, beginning with a hexagon as a whole. Have them decide what fraction of a hexagon the other shapes represent.

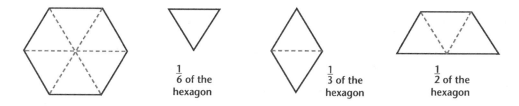

$\frac{1}{6}$ of the hexagon     $\frac{1}{3}$ of the hexagon     $\frac{1}{2}$ of the hexagon

**Directions**

Have students use terms—such as 'quarter turn', 'half turn', 'three-quarter turn', 'right' and 'left'—to give and follow directions for walking around the classroom. Ask: If one whole turn means you end up facing the same direction as you began, what fraction of the turn will have you facing the opposite direction? Explore with students different ways of recording the directions. Relate the rotational movements to the minute hand on an analogue clock.

KU **3**

# Middle ✔✔

### Sharing Sweets

Show the class 20 sweets. Ask: If I ate five sweets, what fraction of the sweets have I eaten? Some people in the class say one quarter; some say one fifth. Who is right?

### Fraction Machine

Extend the Beginning Sample Learning Activity, 'Function Box' (Key Understanding 1) by asking the machine to make four fifths of different collections and/or objects.

### Fraction Words

Have students draw their interpretations of fraction words used in context. For example, say: I need two and three quarter cups of self-raising flour to make scones. Adam ate one and three quarter sandwiches. You only left two and a quarter packets of sweets for the party. I've got two thirds of the chocolate bar left. One and a half classes can fit on the bus. You'll need to leave at least two and a half pages in your notepad to finish that work.

# SAMPLE LEARNING ACTIVITIES

## Later ✔✔✔

### Sharing Sweets

Organise students into different-sized groups. Then, ask students to share equally various quantities of sweets (a jelly snake, a packet of ten chocolate frogs, a bag of jelly beans and a box of popcorn) among their groups. Have each group chart the results using diagrams and fractional language. Make a classroom display of the charts. Ask students to discuss the variations in parts and wholes, in relation to the fraction names used.

### Measuring Fractions

Invite students to use measuring tools (e.g. scales, rulers, grid paper, measuring jugs). Ask them to find a fraction (e.g. two thirds, three fifths) of a range of 'wholes' (e.g. a unit on a number line, a piece of string, a few straws, some rice, paper circles). Have them record what they did and the result in words, diagrams and numerals. Ask: What is the same in each case?

### Fractions and Shapes

Ask students to use pattern blocks, beginning with a trapezium as a whole. Have them decide what fraction of a trapezium the other shapes represent. For example, ask them to show the hexagon as $\frac{2}{1}$ of the trapezium. Be sure to draw out the link between the denominator and the unpartitioned 'whole' trapezium, and the numerator and the two trapeziums in the hexagon. Invite students to find, record and explain other fraction relationships among the blocks.

### Finding Wholes

Give students pattern blocks to find the whole shape when a triangle represents one third (quarter, sixth, twelfth). Ask students to record these as diagrams and use fraction symbols.

### Fractional Values

Ask students to use pattern blocks to make a pattern. Then, have them refer to their entire pattern as a whole unit. Ask students to find the fractional value of each piece as it relates to the whole pattern and justify their conclusions.

# Later ✔✔✔

### Stars

Invite students to show and explain how a fraction, such as two thirds, means two out of every three. Have students examine a range of diagrams and say which diagrams show that two thirds of the stars are black. Ask: Why do you think that?

### Parts of a Whole

Ask students to find parts of a whole where the whole itself is a part of something else. For example, say: Three quarters of a pie was left in the fridge. Six students are supposed to share the pie. What fraction of the piece of pie is each portion? What fraction of the whole pie is each portion? Draw a diagram to show your answer. Encourage students to use fractional numbers in their diagrams.

### Understanding Fractions

Invite individual students to explain to the class what they think the term 'fraction' means and to illustrate what they understand about a particular fraction, such as three quarters. Ask: If you were helping your younger brother with his homework and he asked you what a fraction is, what would you say? Then, say: Show him what three quarters means in as many ways as you can using materials or pencil and paper.

### Three Quarters

Have students sort illustrations into two categories: those which can be represented by three quarters and those that can't. Ask students to explain their choices.

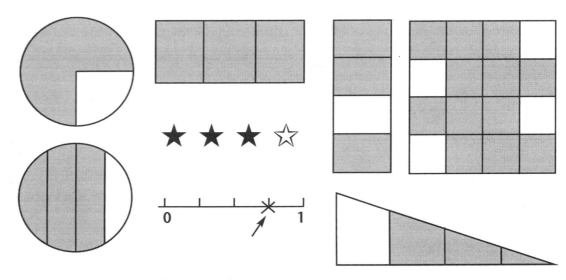

### Fractions and Facts

Give students a selection of newspaper and magazine articles and advertisements. Then, ask students to find examples of fractions. Invite students to explain how each fraction is used and then write in words what the numerator and denominator represent. For example: the number of tickets sold for a concert over the total number of seats in the concert venue. Use the information given to check the accuracy of the fraction used, or to work out the actual numbers, or the quantities the fractions represent. Encourage students to write to newspaper and/or magazine editors to ask for more information where appropriate.

### Thirds

Ask students to group several different-sized collections into three equal parts; for example, six grapes, 12 sultanas and 18 nuts. Invite students to name the parts. Say: These are all thirds. Why don't they have the same quantity? How can one third be more than another third? Repeat this type of activity for other fractional parts.

### Fractions of a Metre

Extend later sample learning activity 'Million Square' by inviting students to explore fraction relationships within a square metre. For example: *A square decimetre is one hundredth of the area of one metre. A square millimetre is one millionth of the square metre. A single millimetre strip down the side of the square metre is one ten thousandth of the square metre.* (see Understand Whole and Decimal Numbers, Key Understanding 8 and Sample Lesson 4).

KU 3

## KEY UNDERSTANDING 4

*The same fractional quantity can be represented with a lot of different fractions. We say fractions are equivalent when they represent the same number or quantity.*

Students will come to understand that one half, two fourths and four eighths are different ways of representing the same quantity, and that every fraction has an infinite number of equivalent forms. When a fraction represents a quantity or number, we imagine a whole object or a collection and think of partitioning it successively. Two fractions are equivalent if they represent the same amount of the relevant whole. Thus, we say 'one third' is equal to 'two sixths' because partitioning the same object or collection into three, then six parts shows it to be so. The fraction 'one third' means not simply one out of three parts, but 'one out of each three parts'. Finding one third of a particular quantity is the same as finding two sixths of it.

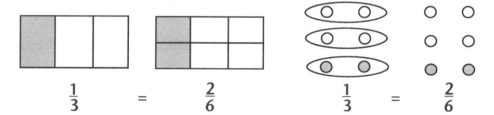

$$\frac{1}{3} \quad = \quad \frac{2}{6} \qquad\qquad \frac{1}{3} \quad = \quad \frac{2}{6}$$

Students can often be taught fairly quickly to produce equivalent fractions by rote. However, they may have little understanding of what they are doing or why, and so they forget just as quickly. The result is that they have to be taught this over and over again, year after year.

A slower, but surer, process based on extensive experience with partitioning quantities is likely to promote more sustained learning. So, students should find equivalent fractions by physically or mentally re-partitioning materials. The goal should be to visualise fractional parts. Only later, should students generalise to a technique for producing equivalent fractions by computation when visualising is difficult.

Students who have achieved Level 3 of the outcome can describe easily modelled or visualised fractional equivalences in words. For example, they may say that a third of the pizza is the same as two lots of one sixth of it, and record this as: *1 third = 2 sixths*. At Level 4, students do this for the range of common fractions and can express the results symbolically: $\frac{1}{3} = \frac{2}{6}$. They will use easily visualised equivalences to compare two fractions, saying which is bigger.

At Level 5, students can generate equivalent fractions for a given symbolically presented fraction, such as $\frac{3}{5}$. They can also choose the appropriate equivalent fraction for particular situations, such as comparing two fractions or adding them. That is to say, students can choose a suitable common denominator.

As described in Key Understanding 7, the fraction symbol is also sometimes used to describe a ratio or proportional relationship between two quantities, such as when describing concentrations in mixtures or scales. Equivalent fractions can also be found for these types of fractions.

KU 4

# SAMPLE LEARNING ACTIVITIES

## Beginning ✔

### Equal Parts

Challenge students to think about fraction equivalences as they play with models partitioned into equal parts. For example, as they play with fraction cakes, say: You have two quarters of a cake. I have half a cake. Do we have the same amount of cake? Who has more?

### Comparing Fractions

Organise students into groups of three. Then, give each group three strips of paper that are equal in length. Ask them to fold one strip in half, one in quarters and one in eighths. Have students draw in the fold lines, then determine the number of equal parts in each strip. Invite students to compare their strips and say what is different and what is the same about them. Introduce fractional language to show that one whole strip can be two halves, four quarters or eight eighths.

### Fraction Circles

Ask students to compare fractions using three paper circles that are equal in size. Have them fold, mark and then cut one circle into halves, one into quarters and one into eighths. Have students match the pieces to determine how many quarters and eighths fit exactly on a half circle. Later, repeat this activity with paper rectangles. Ask: What stays the same? What is different?

### Halves and Quarters

Have students compare two sandwiches of the same size. For example: ▢ and ⊞. Say: I have one piece of the first sandwich and you have two pieces of the second one. I think you've got more because you've got two pieces and I've only got one. What do you think? Invite students to explore different ways to cut paper squares into halves and quarters to answer the question: Are two quarters always the same amount as one half? (See 'Pets' Middle Sample Learning Activity, Key Understanding 2, and Sample Lesson 2, page 109.)

### Fractions of Collections

Ask students to compare the number of sweets in a half share of one collection of eight sweets with the number of sweets in two quarter shares of another collection of eight sweets. Ask: How does this change if one collection has 12 sweets instead of eight? If two quarters is the same amount as one half, why is it that two quarters of eight sweets is not the same number as one half of twelve sweets?

## SAMPLE LEARNING ACTIVITIES

## Middle ✔✔

### Representing Fractions

Organise students into pairs. Ask them to use identical paper shapes to make a chart that shows some of the ways any given fractional amount could be represented. Be sure to increase the level of difficulty to match students' current level of understanding. Introduce the idea of equivalence so that students can record their practical representations using fractional language. For example: *I folded my square into eight and coloured four squares. Four eighths is the same amount as one half.*

### Equivalent Fractions

Invite students to use materials (e.g. strips of paper, fraction cakes, pattern blocks) to find as many different fractions as they can that are equivalent to one half. Repeat this activity with one third and one quarter, then two thirds and three quarters. Ask students to discuss and justify their results.

### Fraction Circles

Ask students to compare fractions using four paper circles that are equal in size. Have them fold, mark and then cut one circle into halves, one into quarters, one into eighths, and one into sixteenths. Have students explore equivalent fractions by matching sections of the circles. Later, extend this activity using suitable models (e.g. paper rectangles and strips of paper) to find equivalent fractions for thirds, fifths, sixths, ninths and tenths.

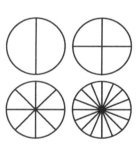

### Equivalence

Pose this situation to the class: Andrew said, 'Three quarters equals six eighths!' Angela said, 'Not always, it depends!' Ask students to explore the equivalence and to explain how both students can be right. Have them find a way to illustrate an equal and an unequal representation using materials of their choice. Draw out the idea that for three quarters to be equivalent to six eighths, the wholes must be the same.

### Chocolate Bars

Ask students to use grid paper representations of chocolate bars to investigate questions, such as: Jackie has two thirds of a chocolate bar and Martin has eight twelfths of the same size chocolate bar. Who has more chocolate, or do they both have the same amount? Explore if this is still true for different-sized and shaped chocolate bars when the wholes are the same and when the wholes are different.

KU 4

# Middle ✔✔

### Marbles

Have students find equivalent fractions of collections, such as half a bag of marbles compared to two quarters of the same bag of marbles. Ask: How can you have the same amount of marbles both times? Ask students to investigate other equivalent fractions for a particular sized bag of marbles. Ask: What is the same about half, two quarters and three sixths? What is different?

### Equivalent Fractions

Ask students to fold paper strips, which are equal in length, into halves, thirds, quarters, sixths, eighths and twelfths, then label the sections. Have students line up the strips to find equivalent fractions. Discuss how accuracy is important if the strips are to give useful information.

| $\frac{1}{2}$ | | | | | | $\frac{1}{2}$ | | | | | |
|---|---|---|---|---|---|---|---|---|---|---|---|

| $\frac{1}{3}$ | | | | $\frac{1}{3}$ | | | | $\frac{1}{3}$ | | | |
|---|---|---|---|---|---|---|---|---|---|---|---|

| $\frac{1}{4}$ | | | $\frac{1}{4}$ | | | $\frac{1}{4}$ | | | $\frac{1}{4}$ | | |
|---|---|---|---|---|---|---|---|---|---|---|---|

| $\frac{1}{6}$ | | $\frac{1}{6}$ | | $\frac{1}{6}$ | | $\frac{1}{6}$ | | $\frac{1}{6}$ | | $\frac{1}{6}$ | |
|---|---|---|---|---|---|---|---|---|---|---|---|

| $\frac{1}{8}$ | | $\frac{1}{8}$ | | $\frac{1}{8}$ | | $\frac{1}{8}$ | | $\frac{1}{8}$ | | $\frac{1}{8}$ | $\frac{1}{8}$ | $\frac{1}{8}$ |
|---|---|---|---|---|---|---|---|---|---|---|---|

| $\frac{1}{12}$ | $\frac{1}{12}$ | $\frac{1}{12}$ | $\frac{1}{12}$ | $\frac{1}{12}$ | $\frac{1}{12}$ | $\frac{1}{12}$ | $\frac{1}{12}$ | $\frac{1}{12}$ | $\frac{1}{12}$ | $\frac{1}{12}$ | $\frac{1}{12}$ |
|---|---|---|---|---|---|---|---|---|---|---|---|

### Fractions of a Collection

Invite students to find different fractions of a collection and to say which result in the same amount and which do not. For example, say: Find a third, then two sixths, then a quarter, then four twelfths of a dozen eggs. How many eggs do you have for each fraction? Why did some of the different fractions result in the same number of eggs? Explain why this happened.

### Did You Know?

**A diagnostic activity for the beginning and middle years**

Ask students to sit in groups. Give each group several 'sandwiches' of the same size drawn on sheets of paper: some divided into two pieces and others divided into four pieces. Ask students to take a half a sandwich each.

- Do students accept two of the quarters as half a sandwich?
- Do students think their piece is a 'half'?
- Do students think each of the halves has exactly the same amount of bread?

For some students, the connection between half and two is so strong that they believe you can only have halves if the whole is divided into exactly two pieces. Students may be prepared to call each rectangle in the first diagram a half and each triangle in the second a half. However, they may not see immediately that the rectangle is the same size as the triangle.

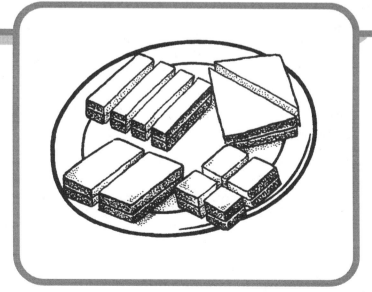

KU 4

# SAMPLE LEARNING ACTIVITIES

## Later ✔✔✔

### Bags of Marbles

Invite students to explore fraction representations using bags of marbles. Have them begin with a bag of 12 marbles and establish what fraction of the bag one marble would be, then write two, three, four, up to 12 marbles as fractions of the bag. Then, challenge students to find all the fraction equivalents possible with denominators between 1 and 12. Later, have students repeat the process with a bag of 24 marbles. Then, ask them to do the same with 36 marbles. Have them compare the lists of equivalent fractions from the three bags. Ask: Which fraction equivalents are the same in each? How can you explain this when there are different numbers of marbles in the bags?

### Fraction Tapes

Have students make paper fraction tapes to explore equivalent fractions. Ask them to join four equal lengths of paper and label them in halves, from 0 to 4. Encourage students to use both mixed and improper fraction notation for each part; for example: $1\frac{1}{2}$ and $\frac{3}{2}$. Then, ask them to make tapes, which are equal in length, for thirds, quarters, sixths and eighths. Have students use the tapes to compare and combine fractions to a total of 4. Ask: Which fraction tape shows a fraction equivalent to $2\frac{1}{2}$? Which fraction tape would show the result of adding a third of a strip to one and a half strips? If I took a half of a strip away from two and two thirds strips, how much is left? What new tape would I need to make to add three quarters of a strip to one third of a strip? Encourage students to justify their responses.

### Equivalent Fractions

Ask students to partition a whole into increasingly smaller parts to generate equivalent fractions. Have them devise and discuss rules for generating sequences of equivalent fractions. Draw out the idea that there can be an infinite number of equivalent fractions.

### Chocolate

Build on the Later Sample Learning Activity, 'Chocolate Bars', in Key Understanding 6. After students have formulated a general rule for finding divisions, such as $3 \div 4$, ask them the result of a simple example, such as $2 \div 3$. Emphasise that this means 'two things shared between three'. Then, ask students to predict what they would get if they shared four things between six people. Some students might use their new rule and give an answer of $\frac{4}{6}$. Other students might say that it is the same answer as two shared between three. Have students use diagrams to explore the idea. Draw out the idea that this shows $\frac{4}{6} = \frac{2}{3}$.

### Rolling Dice

Label each face of a die with one of these fractions: $\frac{1}{4}, \frac{2}{6}, \frac{4}{5}, \frac{1}{6}, \frac{2}{3}, \frac{6}{10}$. Then, label each face of a second die with one of these fractions: $\frac{1}{3}, \frac{2}{12}, \frac{3}{5}, \frac{8}{10}, \frac{4}{6}, \frac{2}{8}$. Each student takes turns to roll the dice. To make a move, that student has to decide whether the fractions shown are equivalent or not. Ask students to give reasons for their decisions.

### Relay Race

Have students work out how many runners are needed for a relay race if each person runs an eighth of one kilometre and the race is three quarters of a kilometre long. Ask students to draw a diagram Ask: How many runners are needed for one quarter of a kilometre? How does knowing this help you to solve the problem?

### Fraction Problem

Pose this problem to students: Two students were discussing fractions. Saeed said, 'Two fourteenths is double one seventh.' Wendy said, 'No, it isn't. They are the same size.' Who do you think is right? Have students draw a diagram to justify their answer, then share their results with a partner.

### Pizza Fractions

Ask students to make models of half a pizza and a third of a same size pizza. Then, have students place the two sections together. Ask: What fraction of a whole pizza are these pieces put together? Have students draw partitions onto a series of other whole pizzas, into fifths, sixths, up to twelfths and place the fraction sections onto these to decide which partitions are most helpful. Draw out the idea that the pizza partitioned into sixths is the most helpful for adding halves and thirds. (See also Later Sample Learning Activity, 'Pizza', in Calculate, Key Understanding 7.)

KU 4

## KEY UNDERSTANDING 5

*We can compare and order fractional numbers and place them on a number line.*

Fractions are often used to describe quantities (e.g. three quarters of an apple, three quarters of a metre), but they also represent numbers (the number 'three quarters') that have their own properties and their own position on a number line. For example, 'a number between 2 and 3 and closer to 3' is an approximate description of the position of the number 'two and three quarters'. We can compare and order fractions and place them on a number line just as we can whole and decimal numbers. (See also Understand Whole and Decimal Numbers, Key Understanding 8.)

Students should count in fractional amounts; for example, half, one, one and a half, two, two and a half, and so on). They will begin to develop a sense of the relative magnitude and position of easily visualised fractions, such as three quarters, and one and two thirds. Students should be helped to develop the capacity to 'see' in their mind's eye where three quarters will be on a number line and where seven eighths will be and so conclude that $\frac{3}{4}$ is less than $\frac{7}{8}$. They should also understand that this supposes a common 'whole', and why one quarter of a particular whole is always less than one half of it. However, a quarter of one whole (an extra large pizza) may be bigger than a half of another (a medium pizza).

Students should develop a repertoire of strategies for comparing and ordering fractions such as the following.

- Compare each fraction to a 'benchmark' number (often $\frac{1}{2}$ or 1); for example, $\frac{1}{3}$ is smaller than a half and $\frac{5}{8}$ is bigger than a half, so $\frac{1}{3} < \frac{5}{8}$.

- Think about each fraction's distance from 1; for example, eighths are smaller than fifths, so $\frac{7}{8}$ is closer to 1 than $\frac{4}{5}$. Therefore, $\frac{7}{8}$ is bigger than $\frac{4}{5}$.

- Find each as a fraction of a suitable number and compare how many you get; for example, to compare $\frac{4}{7}$ and $\frac{3}{5}$, think of a number both denominators 'go into' (35). $\frac{4}{7}$ of 35 is 20 and $\frac{3}{5}$ of 35 is 21, so $\frac{3}{5}$ is more.

Students who have achieved Level 3 can place unit fractions in order and justify the order using materials, diagrams or words. By thinking of four fifths as 'four lots of one fifth', these students also see that four fifths of a quantity will be more than three fifths of it. However, they may not recognise this symbolically.

Students who have achieved Level 4 can order fractions involving easily visualised or well-known equivalences, saying, for example, that two thirds is more than a half. They may, however, find it difficult to come up with an appropriate diagram to compare two fractions with different denominators, such as $\frac{2}{3}$ and $\frac{3}{4}$.

Students at Level 5 can draw or visualise diagrams to compare such fractions. They will also choose to express two fractions with a common denominator in order to compare them, or to add and subtract them.

KU **5**

## SAMPLE LEARNING ACTIVITIES

### Beginning ✔

**Counting by Fractions**

Have students carry out counting activities in fractional amounts. For example, ask students to count halved oranges to determine how many whole oranges were cut up (*half, one, one and a half, two, two and a half, …*).

**Ropes**

Stretch a skipping rope across the classroom floor or wall. Mark one end of the rope '0'; the other end '1'. Invite students to stand on or next to the rope to indicate fraction positions, such as half the length of the rope or a quarter. Add a second rope to extend the line to 2 (3) so that students can indicate a position for one and a half lengths of rope. Ask students to explain how they make their decision about where to stand.

**Comparing Halves**

Provide students with two obviously different sized wholes, each split into halves. Ask: Which half would you rather have? Discuss the difference between the halves and why one half is bigger than the other. Ask: Are they both halves? When can halves be different amounts?

## SAMPLE LEARNING ACTIVITIES

# Middle ✔✔

### What Number Am I?

Pose this problem to students: I am less than one but more than zero. I am bigger than one half. Have students guess the number and then discuss the strategies they used to work out the answer. Later, ask them to make up their own fraction clues to give to the class.

### The Frog and the Flea

Pose this problem to students: A frog and a flea had a jumping contest. Each of the frog's jumps was one third of a unit long. Each of the flea's jumps was one quarter of a unit long. The winner was the one who reached four units in the fewest jumps. Predict which creature won and explain why. Encourage students to represent the jumps on a number line to check their predictions. Then, ask: What if the race was longer?

### Fraction Tapes

Help students to see how fractions fit with whole numbers. First, have them fold identical lengths of paper tape into various fractional parts. Then, ask students to label the folds in sequence; for example, from $\frac{1}{4}$ to $\frac{3}{4}$, then label the start '$\frac{0}{4}$' and the end '$\frac{4}{4}$'. Ask: How is the half marked on this tape different from, say, half an apple? Draw out the idea that the fractions on the tape show a position on the tape. (See also Sample Lesson 3, page 137.)

### Pocket Money

Pose this problem to students: Mary and John each spent a quarter of their pocket money. Is it possible for Mary to have spent more money than John? What if they had spent half of their pocket money? Have students justify their responses in terms of the size of the whole.

### Estimating Fractions

Ask students to estimate the size of fractions of things in their environment. For example, say: Show me a third of the whiteboard (your desk, the wall). Ask: How did you decide where a third is?

### Finding Fractions

After activities, such as 'Estimating Fractions', ask students to fold a paper strip to find a given fraction. Give students different-sized strips of paper. Then, ask students to find someone else in the room with the same sized strip and compare fractions. Ask: How do you know that the fractions show the right amount? How can you be sure?

KU **5**

# Middle ✔✔

#### Estimating Positions

Extend the 'Finding Fractions' activity by giving students several strips of paper the same size. Ask them to estimate without folding, the position of a half, a third, a quarter, three quarters and two thirds, each on a different strip. Then, have students place their strips together and review their decisions, making changes to the position of the fractions where appropriate.

#### Cheesecake

Have students think about the size of fractions to solve word problems. For example, say: Dad told Louise and Matthew that there were two pieces of cheesecake left in the fridge. One piece was $\frac{1}{3}$ of the cheesecake. The other piece was $\frac{1}{4}$ of the cheesecake. Dad said the older child should get the bigger piece. He gave Louise $\frac{1}{3}$ of the cheesecake and Matthew $\frac{1}{4}$ of the cheesecake. Who do you think is older: Matthew or Louise? Have students draw diagrams to explain their answers.

#### Fraction Number Line

Draw a number line on the ground or on a large sheet of paper with units and half units marked. Have students jump in units, half units and/or quarter units, counting as they go (e.g. *one quarter, two quarters, three quarters, one, one and one quarter*).

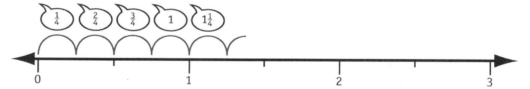

#### Sharing Chocolate

Pose this problem to students: Last night, I was offered the choice of half, a quarter or a third of a chocolate bar. Which one would have been given me the most chocolate? Have students use a number line to justify their responses.

#### Comparing Lengths

Give each student a number line marked in units from 0 to 10. Then, ask students to draw a snake two and a quarter units long. Repeat this activity with a number of different lengths. Have students mark their snakes' positions on the number line and talk about how they determined where the snake would begin and end.

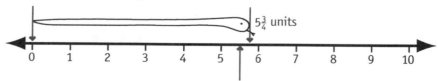

## SAMPLE LEARNING ACTIVITIES

# Later ✔✔✔

### Less Than 100

Ask: What is the biggest number you can think of that is less than 100? Use a long strip of millimetre grid paper to represent a number line segment between 99 and 100. Have students begin by marking $99\frac{1}{2}$ on the strip and then ask them to add numbers larger than this (e.g. $99\frac{3}{4}$). Ask students to indicate and justify the position of their numbers on the line.

### Ordering and Comparing Fractions

Ask students to use a half, a third, a quarter and three quarters as reference points to determine the size of a fraction, or to order and compare fraction numbers. For example, ask: Is $\frac{5}{8}$ smaller or bigger than a half? Does knowing that $\frac{4}{8}$ is a half help? Use what you know to say whether $\frac{8}{14}$ is more or less than $\frac{5}{8}$. Have students use these strategies to order sets of fractions with unlike numerators and unlike denominators; for example: $\frac{2}{3}, \frac{4}{5}, \frac{5}{6}, \frac{9}{10}$.

### Fraction Cards

Have students order sets of fraction cards with:

- like denominators; for example: $\frac{3}{4}, \frac{1}{4}, \frac{2}{4}$; or
- like numerators; for example: $\frac{2}{3}, \frac{2}{5}, \frac{2}{7}$.

Ask them to justify their reasons for ordering the cards as they did.

### Number Lines

Organise students into groups. Ask students to use strips of equal-length card and fold or mark it into fractional parts. Have groups tape their fraction strips together to make separate number lines for halves, thirds, quarters, and so on. Then, ask them to add labels, for example: $\frac{0}{5}, \frac{1}{5}, \frac{2}{5}, \frac{3}{5}, \frac{4}{5}, \frac{5}{5}$ (or 1), then $1\frac{1}{5}$, and so on. Have students use their number lines to count in fractions. For example, say: Begin at one third, then count on by two thirds. Encourage students to compare strips to make other counts. Say: Begin at one and a quarter and count in halves.

### Places on a Number Line

String up a length of string, across the classroom. Add a card labelled '0' at one end and a card labelled '1' at the other end. Ask students to determine where fraction cards would be positioned on the line and justify their suggestions. Draw out the idea that there is a much greater difference between $\frac{7}{8}$ and $\frac{8}{8}$, for example, than there is between $\frac{32}{33}$ and $\frac{33}{33}$ in order to help them understand that $\frac{32}{33}$ must be closer to 1 than $\frac{7}{8}$.

KU 5

# Later ✔✔

### Pocket Money

Pose this problem to students: Felicity and Cameron both got money for Christmas. Felicity said she spent $\frac{1}{4}$ of her money. Cameron said he spent $\frac{1}{5}$ of his. 'You spent more than me!' Felicity added. Cameron replied, 'I couldn't have, a fifth is less than a quarter.' Ask: Could Cameron be right? How could that happen?

### Counting Fractions

Pose this problem to help students count in fractional amounts: I need $1\frac{1}{2}$ metres of braid for the cushion, but I only have a $\frac{1}{10}$ metre ruler. How would I count to measure the braid I need? Have students record the count on a number line.

### Comparing Fractions

Ask students to compare two fractions, such as $\frac{2}{3}$ and $\frac{4}{5}$. Ask: Which number is larger? How do you know? Use a number line to prove that your answer is correct.

### Fraction Problems

Pose this problem to students: Each day, a baker uses $\frac{3}{8}$ of a bag of flour to make bread, and $\frac{1}{4}$ of the same bag of flour to make cakes. Is more flour used to make bread or cakes? Have students use diagrams to show a partner which quantity is bigger.

### Sorting Fractions

Have students explore the relative size of fractions by sorting fraction cards into given categories. For example: less than one or more than one; nearer to zero or nearer to one; nearer to zero, nearer to half or nearer to one. Encourage students to use materials or diagrams to justify how they have sorted their fraction cards.

### Fractions on a Number Line

Ask students to use a number line, marked from 0 to 50, to indicate the position of fractions as numbers as well as fractions of numbers. For example, say: Show the number $\frac{7}{8}$. Show the number that is $\frac{7}{8}$ of 16. Have students compare the language used when referring to fractions as numbers and fractions as operators. Discuss the identity of the whole in each context.

### Estimating

Have students use paper strips of the same length to estimate (without folding to check) the position of a different fraction on each strip. For example, one third on the first strip, one sixth on the second, five sixths, three ninths, seven eighths, and so on. Then, ask students to place their strips of paper one under the other and review their decisions, making changes to their estimates if necessary. Encourage them to check and try other fractions to improve their estimates.

## SAMPLE LESSON 3

**Sample Learning Activity:** Middle—'Fraction Tapes', page 133

**Key Understanding 5:** We can compare and order fractional numbers and place them on a number line.

**Working Towards:** Levels 4 and 5

*It is quite a large mental jump for students to go from thinking of a fraction as part of a given whole, which can either be a single object or a collection of objects, to thinking of fractions as part of the number system.*

KU **5**

## Teacher's Purpose

I gave my Year 5 students part of a number line marked from 0 to 4, then I asked them to show the number 'three quarters' on it. Even though I stressed the word 'number', almost all students showed three quarters of the segment, indicating the section between 0 and 3:

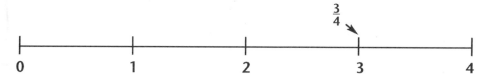

I realised that most of the activities we had been doing this year involved fractions as quantities. So, I decided it was time to provide my students with some experiences involving fractions as numbers.

## Action and Reflection

I began by asking each student to cut four identical strips of paper somewhere between 30 and 50 centimetres long. I asked the students to imagine that each strip of paper represented a journey along a road. The students took one of the strips and folded it at the point on the 'road' where they would take a rest exactly in the middle of their journey. They drew a line across the strip, then I asked, 'So, how far could you say you've come if you began here [pointing to the left end of the strip] and walked as far as here [indicating the mid point]?'

All the students understood that, without knowing the actual distance, we could still say 'halfway'. We labelled the midpoint '$\frac{1}{2}$' and explained the symbols as meaning, 'The trip is in two equal 'part trips', and I've only travelled one part.'

I asked the students what they should write at the end of the strip. Most said one or a whole. However, they did not have an answer when I asked, 'What about if you wanted the number to show that you had split your trip into two equal "part trips"?'

*Length measurement is a useful context for introducing students to the number line representation of the counting numbers. This is also a good basis for developing the idea of fractions as numbers. Eventually, students see that when we refer to fractions as numbers, their 'whole' is the number 1. This means that fraction symbols can be compared and manipulated as objects in their own right.*

Eventually, Jane suggested $\frac{2}{2}$ as showing that two halves are equal to the whole trip. 'The bottom "2" shows the parts and the top "2" shows how many parts we'd travelled,' she said.

Most students then responded correctly with $\frac{0}{2}$ when I asked them what I should write at the start of the strip. They could explain, 'The trip will be in two halves, but this is at the start of it, so we've travelled "zero halves".'

The students were happy to label the parts of the strip in this way. However, I knew they may not have realised that this way of thinking about fractions was somewhat different from their past experiences with quantities.

I asked, 'How is this way of using a half different from when we have, for example, half an apple?' Quickly, I drew an apple on the board, halved it and then shaded one part.

Ivan said, 'It's the same, except on the tape, we have not coloured in the bit to show the journey.'

'So, do we need to colour in the section of the tape?' I asked.

Most students thought that the way we had labelled the tape was fine and that we did not need to colour it. I realised that they still did not see the two ways of thinking about fractions as being different.

'So,' I said, 'What have we labelled as a half on the apple?' I gave them some thinking time and then went on. 'And, what have we labelled as half on our tapes? Is it the same thing?'

'Oh! I see,' said Melissa, 'On the apple, the half shows the bit of apple. On the tape, it shows the spot that is the halfway mark. It doesn't show all of the half.'

Other students around Melissa were nodding, suggesting to me that they could see the difference, so I moved on. 'So, can you find a quarter of the journey on another paper tape?'

## Challenge to Use New Knowledge

The students then made and labelled another strip, representing the same journey, but this time, the journey was divided into four equal 'legs'. After some discussion with their classmates, most students produced a strip that looked like this:

I asked, 'Can you show one quarter of the journey to your partner?' The students easily found the appropriate spot on the tape.

'Now, can you tell your partner how this one quarter is different from one quarter of an apple, or one quarter of a liquorice strap?' I asked.

I quickly changed the diagram of the apple to show a quarter. Then, I drew a piece of liquorice on the board and coloured a quarter of it.

The discussion that followed showed that most students could say the section of the apple was different. However, they struggled with the liquorice strap. But eventually, the students decided that it was the same as the apple because it showed the amount of the liquorice.

'But, you could say that this is the quarter way mark on the liquorice,' said Aaron, pointing to the line where the liquorice had been divided to show the quarters.

'Yes,' said Kylie, 'Then, that would be the halfway mark, and that would be the three-quarter way mark.' She pointed to the other two lines on the drawing.

> *Although the students' language told me they were still tied to the concrete in their thinking about fractions, I felt the way they were using the symbols and the kinds of thinking they were doing showed they were much closer to understanding how fractions fitted within the number system. The direction some students were taking helped me decide on suitable follow-up lessons to further extend their thinking.*

KU 5

## Drawing Out the Mathematical Idea

I thought that this was the appropriate time to make my point, 'Yes, it is like the fractions showing our journey. We could think of the fractions on this tape as numbers on a number line, they show the position of the fraction numbers. They are part of the number sequence. Zero quarters, one quarter, two quarters, three quarters, four quarters. On this one [I pointed to the half tape], it goes zero half, one half, two halves.'

Then, I asked the students to try making the tape to show the journey in eighths. They quickly made this tape by folding and re-folding and labelling. When they had finished, I asked them to count off the sections of the journey as they went past each. I could see that most were accepting of this new idea of fractions and had begun to think of them as part of the number sequence.

I planned to follow this lesson with opportunities to compare the tapes and determine equivalent fractions by matching the fold lines.

## KEY UNDERSTANDING 6

### A fractional number can be written as a division or as a decimal.

The fraction notation developed as a shorthand way to show the division sign, so that $3 \div 4$ became $\frac{3}{4}$. This important relationship between fractions and division is often overlooked by both students and adults. Many will struggle to work out the 'answer' to $3 \div 4$, such as when sharing three chocolate bars among four friends, not seeing immediately that you must get $\frac{3}{4}$ of a bar each.

Investigating the various ways in which, for example, three things can be shared equally among four people, and linking all the resulting portions to the fraction $\frac{3}{4}$, can assist students to use fractions flexibly. It also helps them to understand operations and calculations with fractions. (Link to Calculate, Key Understanding 7.) Thus, the following ways of sharing three pies among four people lead to various ways of getting three quarters of a pie.

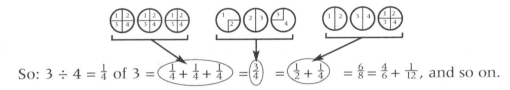

So: $3 \div 4 = \frac{1}{4}$ of $3 = \left(\frac{1}{4} + \frac{1}{4} + \frac{1}{4}\right) = \left(\frac{3}{4}\right) = \left(\frac{1}{2} + \frac{1}{4}\right) = \frac{6}{8} = \frac{4}{6} + \frac{1}{12}$, and so on.

Students can extend this partitioning process to link fractions and decimals. (See also Understand Whole and Decimal Numbers, Key Understanding 7.)

In the previous example, the three pies can be cut into ten equal parts—so that there are 30 tenths in all—and shared among four people, giving seven tenths to each and two tenths left over.

The leftover two tenths can be partitioned into tenths again. This would produce 20 hundredths, which can also be shared among the four people, giving each five hundredths.

So: $\frac{3}{4} = 3 \div 4 = \frac{7}{10} + \frac{5}{100} = 0.75$.

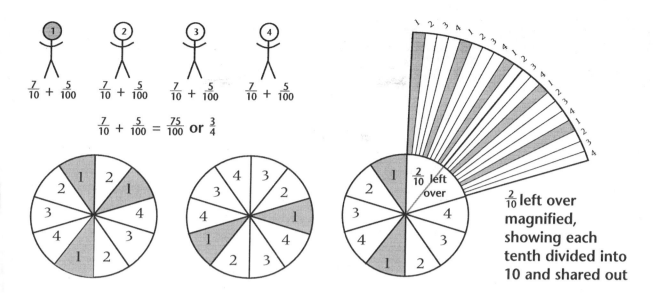

**Three pies shared among four people**

$\frac{2}{10}$ left over magnified, showing each tenth divided into 10 and shared out

This is the essence of the link between fractional and decimal representations of numbers.

Common fractions and decimals are always interchangeable, although, they tend to be more or less helpful in different situations. We often teach students to convert a fraction such as $\frac{3}{4}$ to a decimal by dividing 4 into 3. But this will be quite perplexing to students who have never thought of $\frac{3}{4}$ as equal to $3 \div 4$. Conversely, if students do think of $\frac{3}{4}$ as equal to $3 \div 4$, they will be able to use this immediately to find a decimal equivalent for any fraction by entering $3 \div 4$ into their calculators. What to do will be obvious if they understand fractions in the first place, but it will be meaningless if they do not.

Students who have achieved the outcome at Level 4 link division and fractions and comfortably interchange $2 \div 3$ with $\frac{1}{3}$ of 2 and $\frac{2}{3}$. They can also change between fractions and decimals where the equivalences are easily visualised or drawn (*0.2 is one fifth*). At Level 5, students can use division or some other strategy to move between common fractions and decimals.

**KU 6**

## SAMPLE LEARNING ACTIVITIES

## Beginning ✔

**Sharing**

Have students solve practical sharing problems in which a smaller number of objects is shared among a larger number of people. For example, say: Share these two slices of Fairy Bread among four people. Share three slices among four people. Ask students to demonstrate their results with their slices of bread or paper squares and explain their strategies.

**Linking Decimals and Fractions**

During general classroom interaction and when students are using calculators, make the connection between a half and the decimal notation 0.5. For example, if a student shows 2.5 on the calculator, say: Oh, that's two and a half. Also refer to 50 per cent as equal to half and 100 per cent as equal to a whole in appropriate contexts.

# SAMPLE LEARNING ACTIVITIES

## Middle ✔✔

### Sharing Paper

Organise students into groups of three and then ask them to share one strip of paper. Ask: How much does each person get? Have students record the symbol for the result and show how the problem itself is represented in the number $\frac{1}{3}$. Then, have students explore sharing two strips of paper between three, then three strips and four strips. Challenge students to use what they have found out about fractions to say how much one person gets if ten strips of paper are shared equally among three people.

### Chocolate Bars

Ask students to share a collection of pretend chocolate bars between various numbers of people. Have them record their results using statements such as:

– One bar between two people gives $\frac{1}{2}$ a chocolate bar each.

– Three bars between four people gives $\frac{3}{4}$ of a chocolate bar each.

– Four bars between five people gives $\frac{4}{5}$ of a chocolate bar each.

Invite students to predict what two bars shared between three people will be and then ask them to check. Repeat predicting and then testing until students are able to write their own rule for working out what fraction of a bar each person will get when you know how many bars and how many people there are. (See also Middle Sample Learning Activity, 'Chocolate Bars', in Key Understanding 2.)

### Measurements

When students begin to write decimal notation in measurement activities, incorporate simple fractional language into the discussions. For example, ask: So, you'll have a metre and a half left? Students will begin to link 0.5 to half, 0.25 to a quarter, and so on. They will be exposed to the way simple fractions can be used in context to refer to concrete quantities expressed in decimal fractions. (Link to Understand Whole and Decimal Numbers, Key Understanding 7.)

### Today's Number

Create a set of fraction and decimal cards (e.g. 'half,' $\frac{1}{2}$ ', '0.5') from which students select 'Today's Number'. Discuss where students might see the number written in each way. Ask students to try to find the number in their reading or in the newspaper.

KU 6

# Middle ✔✔

Have students make a set of cards to play 'Concentration'. Students make matching pairs of cards: the first card showing a common fraction; the second, its decimal or percentage equivalent. Ask a student to shuffle the cards and turn them face down on a table in an array. Then, have students take turns exposing a pair of cards. Each student keeps the cards if they match, or turns them face down again if they do not.

| | |
|---|---|
| $\frac{1}{2}$ | 0.5 |
| $\frac{1}{4}$ | 25% |
| $\frac{3}{4}$ | 0.75 |

# SAMPLE LEARNING ACTIVITIES

## Later ✔✔✔

### Chocolate Bars

Ask students to use pretend 'chocolate bars', made from rectangles of paper, to model sharing two bars among three people. Have students record the fraction of a bar each person gets. Repeat for various numbers of chocolate bars and different numbers of people. Draw out the link between division and fractions, for example: 2 bars between 3 people gives $\frac{2}{3}$ of a bar each, so $2 \div 3 = \frac{2}{3}$. Ask: Why does this happen? Does it also work for six bars shared between two people? How about five bars shared between two people?

### Pizza Problems

Pose problems to students to help them relate division to fractional notation: Three pizzas have to be shared equally among four students. How much pizza will each student get? Ask students to draw diagrams to illustrate how they solved the problem, writing their answers as a fraction of a pizza. Then, ask students: Find $\frac{3}{4}$ of one pizza. Find $\frac{1}{4}$ of three pizzas. Invite students to compare and discuss their diagrams and the resulting fractions. Introduce $\frac{3}{4}$ as an alternative to $3 \div 4$ for representing three pizzas shared among four students.

### Fair Shares

Extend the 'Pizza Problems' activity to draw out the idea that if anything is shared between three people, each person gets one third of it. That is, $2 \div 3$ is the same as $\frac{1}{3}$ of 2. Repeat for: $4 \div 5$ is the same as $\frac{1}{5}$ of 4, or $3 \div 4$ is the same as $\frac{1}{4}$ of 3. Rearrange diagrams to show that one third of two identical pizzas is the same amount as two thirds of one of the pizzas. Have students go on to demonstrate why we can say right away that $4 \div 5 = \frac{4}{5}$, $6 \div 2 = \frac{6}{2}$, $4 \div 3 = \frac{4}{3}$, and so on.

### Fifths

Ask students to draw a picture that shows why two fifths of one is the same amount as one fifth of two. Pose this problem: A family of five was left with two chocolate biscuits. Mum said, 'If we share these biscuits, how much do we get each? One child said one fifth; another child said two fifths. Both thought they were right and that the other was wrong. Mum said, 'You could both be right.' Is Mum correct? Focus students' thinking on what each child thought of as the whole.

KU 6

# Later ✔✔✔

### Ways to Share

Extend sharing activities by asking students to share three pizzas between four people in a number of different ways. Each time, have students shade one person's portion, for example:

Then, ask students to write number sentences to describe what they found, for example:

$$3 \div 4 = \frac{3}{4} = \frac{1}{4} + \frac{1}{4} + \frac{1}{4} = \frac{1}{2} + \frac{1}{4}$$

### More Sharing

Brainstorm with students situations where food is sliced into set portions, regardless of the number of shares needed. For example, a whole cake would not be cut into four if only four people were going to eat it. A pizza is often pre-cut into eight portions. A pie is often cut into four. To share the pie between three people, each person would get $\frac{1}{4}$. If they were still hungry, they would then share the remaining $\frac{1}{4}$ of the pie, so: $\frac{1}{3} = \frac{1}{4} + \frac{1}{12}$. Have students use diagrams and numbers to demonstrate this situation and other similar distributions. For example, a large rectangular slice of Lebanese bread is cut into sixths and four students take $\frac{1}{6}$ each. The remaining $\frac{2}{6}$ is then shared, so: $\frac{1}{4} = \frac{1}{6} + \frac{1}{12}$.

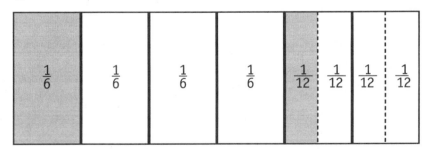

### Fractions to Decimals

Have students carry out activities to explore how decimals are formed from a fraction, such as $\frac{1}{4}$, where the remaining portions have to be continuously shared. For example, say: Start by partitioning a pie, or other wholes, into tenths. Four children take two portions each ($\frac{2}{10}$). Then, the remaining two portions are cut into tenths. The children now have $\frac{20}{100}$ (or $\frac{5}{100}$ each), so: $\frac{1}{4} = \frac{2}{10} + \frac{5}{100} = 0.25$. Have students repeat similar activities by partitioning the pie into tenths to find $\frac{1}{8}$ ($\frac{3}{8}$, $\frac{1}{5}$) of the pie in order to find the equivalent decimal fraction. Ask: If you use your calculators, why do you think you would get 0.3333 and 0.6666 for $\frac{1}{3}$ of the pie and $\frac{2}{3}$ of the pie? (Link to Reason About Number Patterns, Key Understanding 6.)

## Decimal Fractions

Ask students to use square decimetres cut from millimetre grid paper as wholes, in order to show how unit fractions (e.g. $\frac{1}{4}$, $\frac{1}{5}$, $\frac{1}{6}$, $\frac{1}{7}$) can be concretely converted to decimal fractions. Remind students that $\frac{1}{4}$ means $1 \div 4$. Say: Cut the square into tenths, and share the tenths between four people. There are two tenths for each. Then, cut the remaining tenths into ten. These are hundredths. Share the 20 hundredths between four people. There are five hundredths each. Draw out the idea that two tenths and four hundredths is 0.25, so $\frac{1}{4}$ is the same as 0.25. Ask: Which unit fractions can be shared out evenly within four successive sharings (i.e. four decimal places) and which cannot? Predict which fractions will never be shared evenly in tenths no matter how many re-cuttings were carried out. Justify your answers.

## Matching Games

Have students make sets of playing cards made up of pairs or sets of matching common fractions and decimals. Then, have them use the cards to play matching games, such as 'Dominoes', 'Concentration', 'Bingo' and 'Snap'.

## Ordering Collections

Ask students to order collections of cards that show a mixture of common fractions and decimals. Then, invite them to use a number line to indicate the relative position of each, justifying their own answers and challenging other students' placements.

## Measurements

Have students use standard tape measures to record tenths and hundredths on metre-long tapes, which have been folded into simple fraction divisions, labelled and then joined together. Ask students to compare the divisions on their tapes to the decimal notation for metres. Ask: What fractions are recorded at the 1.5 metre mark? How are they the same? How are they different? (See later Sample Learning Activity, 'Fraction Tapes', Key Understanding 4.)

## Fractional Measures

Ask each student to cut a strip of paper exactly one metre long and then fold their strips into halves, quarters, and so on. Have students add labels to each fold with the appropriate fractional measurement. Invite them to use calculators to divide the numerator by the denominator for each fraction and record the resulting decimal fraction. Have students compare their paper strips to metre tapes. Discuss the relationship between the common fractions, decimal fractions and the number of centimetres.

KU 6

**KEY UNDERSTANDING 7**

*A fraction symbol may show a ratio relationship between two quantities. Percentages are a special kind of ratio we use to make comparisons easier.*

Students are usually introduced to the fraction notation as a representation of a quantity or a number. This meaning is important, but it does not capture all the ways that we use fraction notation.

The fraction notation can also be used to represent a proportional relationship between two quantities; for example, when we describe concentrations in mixtures or when we use scales or give test results. Although we are still using the fraction notation, we are not using it to describe a single number or quantity. Rather, we are using it to describe a ratio between two quantities. For example, when we get 7 out of 10 correct on a spelling test, we may write it as $\frac{7}{10}$, but we say it as 'seven out of ten' rather than 'seven tenths'.

Students should understand that to say one of these fractions is bigger than another does not mean it is a bigger quantity. Rather, it is a greater concentration, rate or scale. When such fractions are equivalent, it means that they show the same 'concentration'. However, students should also understand that adding and subtracting these fractions does not generally make sense.

Percentages are generally used in this way. That is, they are used to describe a ratio between two quantities where the 'fraction' has been written with a common denominator of 100. This makes comparisons easy. For example, 'Last week's spelling test was out of 20 and I got 12 right ($\frac{12}{20}$). This week's test was out of 25 and I got 15 right ($\frac{15}{25}$). I got more right this week, but I also got more wrong. Have I improved? Converting each to a fraction of 100, tells us that last week I got 60% right and this week I also got 60% right. I did equally well each week.'

As a general rule, we do not add or subtract percentages because they refer to different wholes. For example, if I get 75% correct on Part A of a test and 75% correct on Part B, then I have 75% correct on the whole test, not 150%. There are circumstances where we set the situation up so that adding does make sense, but generally, it is not appropriate. Thinking about the context is necessary in order to decide what makes sense. Students should derive ratios and percentages from a variety of such situations and explore the ways they can and cannot use them.
(See Backgound notes)

Finding equivalent fractions does make sense in these types of situations. Such fractions are equivalent if they show the same ratio (or 'concentration'). Thus, if a garden spray calls for a one-in-ten concentration, we would have to add 1 litre of concentrate to 9 litres of water, 2 litres of concentrate to 18 litres of water, and so on. The instructions on a 1 litre bottle might say 'add 9 litres of water to the contents of the bottle' or alternatively, say 'add water to make up the quantity to 10 litres'. They mean the same thing in this case and both can be expressed as ratios and written using fractional notation.

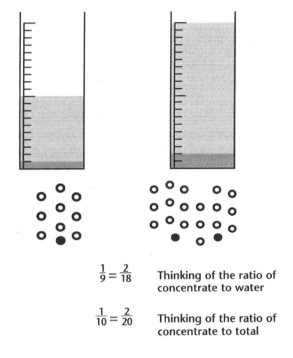

$\frac{1}{9} = \frac{2}{18}$    **Thinking of the ratio of concentrate to water**

$\frac{1}{10} = \frac{2}{20}$    **Thinking of the ratio of concentrate to total**

The use of the fraction notation in the way described here is equivalent to the use of the colon; that is, 2:3 can also be written as $\frac{2}{3}$. While in everyday use, the colon is now more commonly used to record scales and concentrations, the fractional notation can be helpful when we wish to compare such ratios or to calculate with them as in solving proportion problems.

Students who have achieved Level 4 of the outcome can use a ratio to describe straightforward scales and concentrations. They understand what ordering such fractions means and therefore know that one fifth concentrate is stronger than one tenth concentrate. Students who have achieved Level 5 can use fractions as ratios between quantities generally. They also recognise a percentage as a ratio of parts to a whole where the denominator has been made to be 100.

KU 7

## SAMPLE LEARNING ACTIVITIES

### Beginning ✔

Ratio

Introduce ideas about ratio informally, using appropriate language in context. For example, when making lemonade, which needs four scoops of sugar for every two scoops of lemon juice, say: There are two scoops of juice left, so how many scoops of sugar will we need? Repeat for other situations, such as: One car needs four wheels, so how many cars could be made using 12 wheels? (Note: The purpose is of this type of activity is to expose students to situations and questions related to ratio, not to expect accurate numerical answers.)

Percentages

During general classroom discussions, refer to 50 per cent as equal to a half and 100 per cent as equal to a whole in appropriate contexts. For example, while making scones with students that need two cups of flour, after one cup, say: That's half of the flour. We have put 50 per cent of the flour in. Then, after the second cup, say: That's 100 per cent of the flour.

## SAMPLE LEARNING ACTIVITIES

## Middle ✔✔

### Making Jelly

Students make jelly (cordial) using different ratios of water to jelly crystals (cordial concentrate) and say which ratio makes the best jelly (cordial). Say: I have lost the instructions for how to make jelly (cordial). How can we find out the right proportions to make jelly (cordial)? Have students test different concentrations and then decide how they can use fractions to represent the different concentrations. For example, students might say: *I thought the best jelly was made with one packet of jelly crystals and 500 millilitres of water, so that is* $\frac{1}{500}$. Invite students to say what each of the numbers in the fraction represents.

### Feeding the Class

Extend the 'Making Jelly' activity. Ask students to work out how much water and jelly crystals are needed to make enough jelly for the whole class or for the school canteen. Ask: How can we use the fraction to help us work this out?

### Proportional Quantities

Encourage students to use their own methods to solve simple problems involving proportional quantities. For example, say: When visiting the zoo, a pre-primary class needs one adult for every five students. One adult per ten students is needed for the rest of the school. How many adults are needed for the whole school to visit the zoo? Invite students to describe and compare their approaches and then help them to see how the fractions $\frac{1}{5}$ and $\frac{1}{10}$ can be used.

### Proportional Relationships

Ask students to use fractions to represent proportional relationships. Students' answers might include: *I got seven out of ten right in my spelling test, so that makes it* $\frac{7}{10}$. *Half of the class like to eat chips, so that is* $\frac{15}{30}$ *or* $\frac{1}{2}$. Encourage students to read their fractions as, for example, seven out of ten. Ask: Why doesn't it make sense to read this as 'seven tenths'?

### Bargain Hunting

Discuss and explore with students situations such as: If you bought a pair of jeans at a '25% off' sale, what fraction of the full price would you save? What if it was 50% off? What fraction of the full price would you save?

# Middle ✔✔

### Matching Games

Have students make sets of playing cards made up of pairs or sets of matching common fractions and decimals. Include equivalent percentages in the cards; for example, half, $\frac{1}{2}$, 0.5 and 50%. Then, have students use the cards to play matching games. (See also Middle Sample Learning Activity, 'Concentration', and Later Sample Learning Activity, 'Matching Games', Key Understanding 6.)

### Hundred Square

Ask students to use 10 x 10 arrays on grid paper to make equivalent fractions in order to find percentages. For example, to find $\frac{1}{4}$ as a percentage, students use 100 squares, share them out into four groups and then say how many squares in each group. Ask students to represent this as a fraction out of 100 (e.g. $\frac{25}{100}$) and read it as 25 'out of 100'. Draw out the idea that the '%' sign is used to show a ratio 'out of 100'. Then, have students convert the fraction into percentage notation (e.g. 25%). To find $\frac{3}{4}$ as a percentage, students might say how many squares in three of the groups. Have them represent this as a fraction out of 100 and then rewrite it as a percentage. To find out $\frac{12}{20}$ as a percentage, students might share the 100 squares out into 20 groups and say how many are in 12 of them. Have students represent this as $\frac{60}{100}$ and read it as '60 out of 100'. Then, have students write this as '60%'.

# SAMPLE LEARNING ACTIVITIES

## Later ✔✔✔

### Discounts

Have students investigate questions, such as: Would you rather have $\frac{1}{3}$ off the price of something or a discount of 30%? What's a better deal: $\frac{1}{5}$ off the price of something or 50% off? Ask students to justify their choices.

### Units of Measurement

Ask students to investigate the ratios used to represent proportional relationships between different units of measurement. For example, a shortbread recipe might say two cups of flour and six tablespoons of butter. Students could express the relationship as $\frac{flour}{butter} = \frac{2}{6}$. Then, they could generate equivalent fractions to find, for example, how many tablespoons of butter they would need for four (six, one) cups of flour. Ask: How many tablespoons of butter would be needed for seven cups of flour?

### Proportional Relationships

Give students a selection of newspaper and/or magazine articles. Then, ask them to investigate the accuracy with which proportional relationships are expressed in percentages, fractions or decimals. For example, say: This newspaper article states that there was a 34% drop in enrolments at universities in 1998. What might this mean? How would the reporter have calculated this figure? What would we need to know to check this? Does the article give us enough information to do this? If there is not enough information in the article, have students write to the editor and ask for all the data. Invite students to display and share their analyses.

### Sensible Fractions

Pose some problems and have students say when adding fractions makes sense. For example, say:

- Brett ate $\frac{3}{8}$ of the pizza yesterday and $\frac{4}{8}$ today. What fraction of the pizza has he eaten?

- Brett got $\frac{3}{8}$ of the spelling words correct yesterday and $\frac{4}{8}$ today. What fraction of the words has he spelt correctly so far this week?

- $\frac{3}{8}$ of the girls and $\frac{4}{8}$ of the boys walk to school. What fraction of the students walk to school?

- My orange drink was $\frac{3}{8}$ juice to water, and my sister's was $\frac{4}{8}$. What would the concentration of juice be if the drinks were combined? Is it $\frac{7}{8}$, $\frac{7}{16}$, or neither? How do you know? Why can't you add some fractions?

KU 7

# Later ✔✔✔

### Ratios

Invite students to use paper tape to represent ratio situations. For example, say: It takes Andrew five steps to cover the same distance as his dad covers in three steps. Have students work out the ratio of Andrew's steps to his dad's and represent this with a fraction (e.g. $\frac{5}{3}$). Ask: How many steps will Andrew have taken when his dad has taken six (nine) steps? Is the ratio of Andrew's steps to his dad's steps still the same after six steps? Later, have students say why the ratio was written as $\frac{5}{3}$ and not $\frac{3}{5}$. Ask: What would the ratio represent if it was written as $\frac{3}{5}$?

### Making Cordial

Explore dilution ratios with students using white and orange table tennis balls. The white balls represent water; the orange balls represent orange cordial. Invite students to mix different strengths of 'cordial'. Begin with a mixture of three orange and nine white balls. Ask: If I want to keep the taste the same and make more (less) of this drink, what could I do? Have students investigate the pattern, leading to the underlying ratio of one third: one part orange cordial to three parts water. Do the same with a $\frac{15}{20}$ proportion of orange cordial to water. Ask: How could I make more (less)?

### Combining Proportions

Have students decide whether it is sensible to combine proportions. For example, ask: If half the students in one class and a third of the students in a second class are girls, what fraction of the two classes combined are girls? Does it make sense to add a half and a third in the usual way? Why? Why not? Would it make more sense to say one in two students in one class and one in three students in the second class are girls, so altogether two in five ($\frac{2}{5}$) students must be girls? Compare this with the fraction obtained by adding all the girls together for the numerator and adding all the students together to find the denominator. Ask: Are the fractions the same (that is, equivalent)? Why not?

### Matching Games

Invite students to make sets of playing cards made up of pairs or sets of matching common fractions, decimals and percentages. Include equivalent ratios in the cards; for example, two fifths, 0.4, 40%, $\frac{2}{5}$, $\frac{6}{15}$, 4 out of 10. Then, have students use the cards to play matching games. (See also Later Sample Learning Activity, 'Matching Games', Key Understanding 6.)

## Ratio Relationships

Ask students to write fractions to help make comparisons involving ratio relationships in real data. For example, say:

- Find the ratio of teachers to students in primary schools. Then, compare this to the ratio of teachers to students in secondary schools.

- Compare the ratio of pasties to pies sold by the canteen and the local bakery.

- Find out the ratio of notepads to exercise books used in Year 7 compared to Year 1.

Ask: How does writing the ratio as a fraction help you to compare the amounts? Encourage students to use equivalent fractions to make the comparisons easier where necessary.

## Percentages

Have students convert test results (e.g. $\frac{14}{20}$) to percentages using the relationship between the number of items in the test and 100 percentage points. For example, say: If we got all 20 words correct in a spelling test, we'd get 100%. What percentage would we get if we got just one word correct? Would it matter which word we got right? How did you calculate what percentage each word is worth? How does that help you to work out what percentage you got right? What about if there were 25 (50) words? Can you explain how using percentages makes it possible to compare how you performed on the 25-word test with how you performed on the 50-word test?

## Finding Percentages

Ask students to use their calculators to work out the best way of finding percentages. For example, if a sale says 20% off everything, have students compare different methods of working out the new prices of different items. Ask: Why is multiplying the price by 0.8 the easiest way of finding the new price? When told the price of CDs has increased by 10 per cent, why is multiplying by 1.1 the easiest way of finding out the new CD price?

## Hundred Square

Extend the 'Hundred Square' activity (see Middle Sample Learning Activities). Ask students to find the percentage equivalents for fractions such as $\frac{1}{3}$, $\frac{1}{6}$, $\frac{1}{8}$ where there will be remainders that will have to be shared again. For example, for $\frac{1}{8}$, 100 squares partitioned into eight is 12 squares with four squares left over. Partition the leftover squares into tenths. Forty tenths partitioned into eight gives five tenths. So, one eighth is 12 and five tenths out of the 100 squares, which is 12.5%. Later, have students use a calculator to divide the numerator by the denominator and multiply by 100 to find the percentage for any fraction. (Link to the 'Fractions to Decimals' Later Sample Learning Activity, Key Understanding 6.)

KU 7

# BACKGROUND NOTES

## *The Many Meanings and Uses of Fractions*

The most common use of the fraction symbol, as emphasised in schools, is the idea that it represents parts of a single whole. Children are taught that the fraction $\frac{3}{4}$ is essentially an instruction to 'divide the whole into four pieces and take three of them'. While this is a correct use of the fraction notation, it does not convey all the meanings and uses of fractions.

## Fractions as numbers that represent parts of a whole or the result of a division

Children need to develop the flexibility to be able to use fractional numbers such as $\frac{3}{4}$ to describe one portion in each of the following situations:

| | | |
|---|---|---|
| **Three quarters of a single pie**<br><br>A single pie, split into equal parts, take three in every four parts; the portion is three quarters of one pie. | | |
| **Three quarters of a package of party pies**<br><br>A dozen pies, take three in every four of them; the portion is 9 pies. | | |
| **Three pies shared between four people**<br><br>Three pies, shared into parts, take one in every four parts; the portion taken is three quarters of a pie (although it is also one quarter of the three pies). | | |

The common thread that holds these situations together is the idea of fair sharing. By experimenting with situations such as those above, students need to develop the following understandings:

- The fraction $\frac{3}{4}$ describes the result of fair sharing one thing (or collection) into four parts and taking three of the parts. It also describes the result as taking three of the things (or collections), fair sharing the three into four parts and taking one of the parts. These two processes always give, *must* give, the same result. Children need to develop the flexibility to think of these statements as saying the same thing (that is, to see them as equivalent):

$$\frac{3}{4} = 3 \div 4 = \frac{1}{4} \text{ of } 3 = 3 \text{ of } \frac{1}{4} = \frac{1}{4} + \frac{1}{4} + \frac{1}{4}$$

- The fraction $\frac{3}{4}$ describes the result of taking three in every four equal parts. It makes sense that sharing a thing (or collection) into four parts and taking three of them, will produce the same quantity as if we shared the thing into eight parts and took six of them. It also makes sense that 4 people sharing 3 chocolates will get the same amount of chocolate as 8 people sharing 6 chocolates. Children need to understand that the two fractions $\frac{3}{4}$ and $\frac{6}{8}$ are equivalent. Within this meaning of fractions, equivalent fractions describe the same amount of the whole or collection.

When we use fractions in the ways described in this section, we are thinking of the fraction as a number or as representing a given quantity. We can place these numbers on a number line, compare and order them and add, subtract, multiply and divide them.

## Fractions as pairs of number that represent the ratio between two quantities

The fraction notation can also be used to represent a proportional relationship between two quantities such as when we receive 7 out of 10 for a spelling activity and write it as $\frac{7}{10}$. In this case, 7 is a number and so is 10, but $\frac{7}{10}$ is not. Indeed, we would usually say this as '7 out of 10' rather than seven tenths.

We also use fractions to show a proportional relationship when we describe concentrations in mixtures, for example, in gardening or cooking or when we indicate scales. In such cases, although we are still using the fraction notation, we are not using it to describe a single number or quantity but rather to describe a ratio between two quantities.

Adding and subtracting these fractions does not generally make sense. For example, we may get 7 out of 10 ($\frac{7}{10}$) and 6 out of 10 ($\frac{6}{10}$) in successive rounds of a game or in two parts of a test. The total would be 13 out of 20 ($\frac{13}{20}$) and not $\frac{13}{10}$ which is what we would get if we added $\frac{7}{10}$ and $\frac{6}{10}$ as though each was a number. Similarly, if we were to put together two batches of pastry each containing one third of butter to flour, we would NOT add one third to one third to get two thirds. Rather, the total batch would still have one third of butter to flour. More information about ratio is provided in Key Understanding 7.

**CHAPTER 5**

# Number Level Statements

**Level 1** Number Level Statements

## Cluster Level Description

Students who have achieved Level 1 can read, write and say small whole numbers, say how many things there are, make collections of a given size, and describe order. The student visualises number stories, partitioning small numbers and representing them with materials, drawings, a calculator or with role play. The student mentally solves self-generated or orally presented questions from stories.

## Elaboration

### Understand Numbers

Students can count. This means that they can say the counting numbers in order and use these numbers to decide, for example, that there are six forks on the table so they need to find six knives in the drawer to go with them. They will match the numbers in order as they point to and look at each object exactly once, and they know that the last number said tells 'how many'.

Nevertheless, many students who have attained Level 1 of the outcome may still think that if they start counting in a different place they will get a different answer. They may not fully trust the count and so may choose not to count. For example, students who can count when asked to find 'how many' or when the word 'count' is stated, may not choose 'counting' to help them decide if there are enough drinks for everyone in a group. Instead, these students may hand out the drinks or match a person's name to each drink—or guess.

Students can use numbers to order things; for example, they can point to the fifth person in a row and they understand the difference between 'five things' and 'the fifth thing'. They also know that if they have eight cards and their friend has ten, then their friend has more cards. When numbers are beyond their immediate experience, they may lose confidence in this 'property' of the counting numbers. For example, they might not be convinced that a friend's collection of 27 cards has more than their collection of 25 cards, even if they can 'count' that far.

Students can recognise small collections by seeing at a glance how many there are without counting (that is, subitising). They can think of small numbers as composed of other numbers; for example, seven can be thought of as a five pattern (⦂•⦂) and a two pattern (⦂), and five counters as three red and two blue.

Students know that money is used to buy things and that if you have insufficient money you can't buy something, whereas if you give too much money, you should get change. They may not recognise particular coin values but are aware that coins are worth different amounts—although many still believe that more coins means more money.

### Understand Operations

Students can draw pictures, act out or use materials to illustrate number stories. For example, when told a story that three chickens came home and then two more chickens came, they can imagine or model the situation and say that five came home altogether. Students can do this for self-generated or orally presented stories involving small, easily visualised numbers.

### Calculate

Students use mental imagery and mental counting strategies to add and subtract small numbers, such as 3 and 4, where the numbers occur in 'stories' involving small numbers or are in easily visualised situations.

## Level 2 Number Level Statements

### Cluster Level Description

Students who have achieved Level 2 can read, write, say and count with whole numbers to beyond 100, comparing and describing collection sizes. They understand 'half' and 'quarter', splitting quantities into equal shares. These students understand and make the connections between counting, number partitions, addition and subtraction, and use them to represent situations involving all four basic operations. They use mental strategies when adding one-digit numbers and calculators for two-digit numbers.

### Elaboration

#### Whole and Decimal Numbers

These students use the decades (10, 20, 30, 40, 50, and so on) to count into the hundreds without assistance to at least 210. They can count backwards and forwards independently from any number to 100. While students at this level can read two-digit numbers, they may sometimes write numbers incorrectly. For example, they may write 6004 for 'six hundred and four'.

Students now trust and use counting themselves. They know that any collection has only one 'count'. They are convinced that a collection of 48 always has more in it than a collection of 45, and that alternative strategies for counting a collection should produce the same result; for example, counting in threes always gives the same result as counting in ones.

Students at Level 2 recognise the values of coins and can count coins to decide how much money they have and whether or not they have enough money to buy something.

#### Fractions

While recognising that in social situations (e.g. family meals) fair shares may not be equal, students also understand the notion of 'fair' when used to mean 'equal shares'. Students use a variety of strategies (e.g. symmetry, dealing out, weighing) to partition quantities into two equal shares and then name each share a 'half'. They produce partitions into halves themselves and link the action of splitting into two equal parts with the language of 'halving'. Students may not yet be able to get the parts quite right, but they know that the parts should be equal. They recognise half of a half as 'a quarter' and some students may even partition again to form eighths. Thus, they can find one quarter of a pie by halving it and then halving it again, and separate the class into four quarters by 'sharing' class members into four teams.

## Understand Operations

Students at Level 2 link various problems to the addition and subtraction operations. They understand what addition and subtraction mean, they write sensible story problems and use the range of everyday expressions for addition and subtraction (e.g. 'subtract', 'take away', 'difference').

Students know that although a quantity has only one 'count', it can also be thought of as composed of parts. For example:

| 7 | 4 |
|---|---|
| 11 ||

**So, 7 + 4 and 4 + 7 = 11 and 11 − 4 = 7 and 11 − 7 = 4**

This enables students to see why a problem, which they think of as being without adding but with one of the addends unknown, can be solved by subtracting, or vice versa.

These students recognise that subtraction is useful for apparently different types of problems. For example, students know that these problems can be solved by working out 17 − 9: 'I had 17 cards and lost 9. How many cards do I have left?'; 'She has 17 cards and I only have 9. What's the difference?'; 'I need 17 cards, I but only have 9. How many more do I need?'

Students at this level are beginning to understand what multiplication means. They model problems involving 'repeating equal quantities' with materials and diagrams. For example, 'For each flower, we will need five petals. How many petals do we need for three flowers?' However, students are likely to think of this situation as repeated addition (5 + 5 + 5). Given access to calculators, they may think of the ☒ sign on the calculator as a shortcut way of telling the calculator to add three lots of five.

Students use materials and diagrams to represent sharing and grouping situations involving whole numbers. They solve simple division problems, such as 'How many lots of 7 in 28?' However, their thinking may be on the basis of counting and/or subtracting equal quantities. They may not connect sharing with grouping situations, not recognising, for example, that 15 ÷ 5 can represent '15 things shared into five groups' and also 'how many fives in 15?'

### Calculate

Students count on instead of counting all to find the result of combining two quantities. They remember many basic addition (to 10 + 10) and subtraction facts. They also have some strategies to help them calculate other additions and subtractions. They may mentally find 7 + 9 by using known facts; for example: *7 + 9 is the same as 8 + 8, which is 16.* Students also use the patterns in the way we write numbers to help them calculate. For example, they may find 40 + 80 mentally by thinking about the sum as: *8 tens and 4 tens makes 12 tens, which is 120.* They know that it often makes sense to rearrange the parts of an addition for whole numbers.

Students can now partition into tens and ones to add and subtract two-digit numbers. They subtract larger numbers, such as 37 from 64, using physical materials, diagrams, calculators, or informal pen-and-paper methods. For example, they might draw jumps along a number line, from 37 to 40 to 50 to 60 to 64, and then add the 'jumps' (3 + 10 + 10 + 4).

These students estimate in simple ways to check two-digit addition and subtractions. For example, saying that 16 + 19 cannot be 25 because it has to be more than 30.

# Level 3 Number Level Statements

## Cluster Level Description

Students read, write, say, count with and compare whole numbers into the thousands and read, write, say and understand the meaning of unit fractions. They use the understanding of the meaning, use and connections between the four operations on whole numbers to choose appropriate operations. These students add, subtract whole numbers and money, multiplying and dividing by one-digit whole numbers, using mostly mental strategies for doubling halving, adding to 100, and additions and subtractions readily derived from basic facts.

## Elaboration

### Whole and Decimal Numbers

Students who have achieved Level 3 use the patterns in the way we write and say numbers to read, write and say numbers into the thousands and to partition these numbers in standard ways. They know, for example, that 2354 is 2000 + 300 + 50 + 4 and that it is said as 'two thousand, three hundred and fifty-four'. They also write correctly orally presented numbers, such as 'seven hundred and sixty-four' as 764 (rather than, say, 70064).

Students also partition two-digit numbers in non-standard ways. They know, for example, that 37 can be represented as: *3 tens and 7 ones* as well as *2 tens and 17 ones, 1 ten and 27 ones*, or *37 ones*. Students can also count forwards in 10s, from any number (e.g. 16, 26, 36, 46). They use the decimal form to make sense of measurements and money. For example, they understand that 3.56 metres is a bit more than three-and-a-half metres, and can rewrite it as 3 metres and 56 centimetres. They also interpret calculator displays involving money and measurements; for example, reading 45.9 on a calculator display as $45.90.

### Fractions

At Level 3, students have generalised their knowledge of partitioning into two parts to the idea of partitioning into two, three, four, five or more equal groups. They can partition and rearrange collections and objects in a variety of ways to show equal parts. Students now accept that the parts can look different, but still be equal in size. They link the action of sharing into equal number of portions with the language of unit fractions, saying, for example, that there are six equal parts and so each part is 'one sixth'. They count orally in unit fractions (e.g. one third, two thirds, three thirds or one, one and one third), write these numbers in the same way (perhaps, 1 third, 2 thirds, one) and record them on a paper strip or number line.

Students also write and recognise $\frac{1}{3}$, $\frac{1}{5}$, $\frac{1}{6}$, $\frac{1}{7}$, and so on, but they may not consistently write, for example, two thirds as $\frac{2}{3}$.

Students can describe easily modelled or visualised fraction equivalences in words. For example, they may say that a third of the pizza is the same as two lots of one sixth of it, and record this as: *one third equals two sixths*. They can place unit fractions in order and justify the order using materials, diagrams or words.

### Understand Operations

Students at Level 3 use the range of alternative everyday expressions for the four basic operations interchangeably (e.g. 'lots of', 'product', 'groups', 'times', 'multiply', 'divide').

Students deal with all the problem types for addition and subtraction in contexts involving large whole numbers. They use the inverse relationship between addition and subtraction routinely for large whole numbers. For example, they readily say: *If 35 + 65 = 100, then 100 – 65 must be 35*.

Students' use of multiplication now extends beyond repeated addition problems to a simple familiar rate ('Apples cost $2.75 a kilogram. How much for four kilograms?'), and combination problems ('I have four shirts and three pairs of pants. How many outfits can I make?'), which do not explicitly involve repeating equal units. However, students' explanations of why multiplication works for these rate and combination problems are likely to draw on ideas about repeated addition.

Students have begun to link the two types of division with its symbolic representation. For example, they can read 45 ÷ 5 = ☐ as 'What is divided by five?' or 'How many fives in 45?'

### Calculate

These students link multiplication and division, for example, using the fact that nine fours are thirty-six (9 x 4 = 36) to decide how many groups of four can be formed in a class of 36 students (36 ÷ 4 = 9). They remember basic addition facts up to 10 + 10, and use these in working out related subtractions and other more complex additions and subtractions mentally. For example, they may say 26 and 19 mentally by saying: *26 + 19 is one less than 26 + 20, so the answer is 45*, or they may break the addition into bits and say: *That's 20 + 10, which is 30 and 9 + 6, which is 15, so the answer is 45*. They might also think of 35 – 17 as *15 + 20 – 17 = 15 + 3 + 18*, or think: *From 17, 3 more makes 20 and 15 more makes 18*. Students remember quite a few basic multiplication facts and use mental methods to work out those they do not remember, or which go beyond the basic facts. For example, knowing four sevens (4 x 7 = 28), they can double to find eight sevens (8 x 7 = 56), and can further say that *8 x 70 is 56 tens, which is 560*.

They understand that it makes sense to rewrite whole numbers as factors and can do this for numbers for which they know the relevant basic facts. They can also further break these facts down into three or four factors and realise that they can do the multiplication in any order and get the same result.

Students use a calculator efficiently for addition, subtraction and multiplication of whole and decimal numbers, including where more than one operation is needed, possibly involving the use of a memory facility. They can also add and subtract simple fractions expressed in words, whole numbers, and amounts of money efficiently and accurately without the use of a calculator. Their methods *may* be standard ones, but they do not have to know standard methods in order to achieve Level 3.

Students estimate both sums and products by rounding to single-digit numbers or simple multiples of 10 and by visualising on a number line, although they may need prompting and support.

**Number Level Statements**

## Cluster Level Description

Students read, write, say, count with and compare whole numbers into the millions and decimals. They also read, write, say and understand the meaning of fractions. These students use understanding of the meaning, use and connections between the operations on whole and decimal numbers to choose appropriate operations. They calculate with whole numbers, money and measures using mostly mental strategies to add and subtract two-digit numbers and for multiplications and divisions related to basic facts.

## Elaboration

### Whole and Decimal Numbers

Students who have achieved Level 4 know that there is a constant relationship between the places in the number system with the values of the positions increasing in powers of 10, from left to right. They use this knowledge to make order of magnitude comparisons between whole numbers. Students understand and use flexibly whole-number place value to partition whole numbers for their own computation and problem solving.

Students interpret large whole numbers, such as those that might appear in a daily newspaper (e.g. $24 567 800). They also understand and use the recurring patterns in each set of three digits (units, thousands, millions) to say and write such numbers for themselves.

Students now understand decimals as numbers, rather than as ways of representing money or measures. They can place decimal numbers (e.g. 0.2, 0.4, 0.6, 0.8, 1.0, 1.2) on a number line. These students read scales, including some in which not every calibration is marked, and order decimals with equal number of places. Students can name the first few places and say that 0.35 is $\frac{3}{10} + \frac{5}{100}$, but they may not be able to use the multiplicative relationship between the places. They can rewrite the decimal part of a number as a fraction; for example, 0.35 is $\frac{5}{100}$.

### Fractions

At Level 4, students interpret fractional qualities as relating to equal parts of something or a collection of things, finding, for example, three quarters of a sheet of paper, a jug of water, or a packet of sweets. They are able to read, write and say common fractions, and have a sense of the relative magnitude of position on a number line of fractions that are easily visualised (e.g. three quarters, two thirds). They can 'see', for example, that $\frac{3}{4}$ is less than $\frac{7}{8}$ relative to a particular 'whole thing', but that $\frac{3}{4}$ of one thing (e.g. their class) may be equal to or more than $\frac{7}{8}$ of another (e.g. the class next door).

Students link fraction and division; for example, they interchange $2 \div 3$ with $\frac{1}{3}$ of 2 and $\frac{2}{3}$. They also move flexibly between fractions and decimals where the equivalences are easily visualised or drawn; for example, 0.2 is one fifth. They can also use a ratio to describe straightforward scales and concentrations, saying, for example, the cordial made with one-fifth concentration is stronger than cordial made with one-tenth concentration.

## Understand Operations

These students use the inverse relationship between addition and subtraction routinely for any numbers including decimals and fractions. They are beginning to understand that multiplication is used for more than repeated addition. For example, they know that $\frac{3}{4}$ x 12 (or 12 x $\frac{3}{4}$) is the same as finding $\frac{3}{4}$ of 12. The fact that they can divide by fractional amounts makes sense to them.

These students will choose to multiply in situations involving familiar everyday rates—such as shopping—and scales. Although, these will tend to involve whole-number multipliers or numbers that they think of as 'like whole numbers'. Students can apply their knowledge of division to situations involving decimals (for money and measurements). They decide whether to add, subtract, multiply or divide in a wide range of practical situations, including where more than one operation is needed.

## Calculate

Students at Level 4 know addition facts to 10 + 10 and multiplication facts to 10 x 10, and derive related subtraction and division facts from them. They use known basic facts to work out those they do not remember. Students try mental arithmetic first for most 'one off' calculations, such as when they need to work out the price of their lunch or what fraction of the class watched a particular television program.

These students have extended their repertoire of strategies for reducing memory load considerably, including those based on standard and non-standard partitioning for calculating mentally in order to give exact values (e.g. *27 x 4 is four twenties, plus four sevens*) or approximate values (e.g. a *quarter of 25 is a bit more than six*).

Students can add and subtract two-digit numbers mentally and multiply and divide mentally by single-digit numbers and multiples of 10 for 'easy' numbers, such as 4 x 32.

These students understand and use pen-and-paper methods to add and subtract numbers that have the same number of decimal places. They can also multiply and divide whole and decimal numbers by single-digit numbers, although, their methods need not be standard ones.

**Level 4**

Students can rewrite larger whole numbers as factors, even into prime factors. They understand why they can rearrange the factors of a number when multiplying and draw freely upon this understanding for their mental calculations. They also make use of calculators to carry out computational tasks, including for writing fractions as decimals. They can interpret remainders when using a calculator for division and use the context, which led to the division, to decide how to round answers and whether an answer makes sense.

Students can estimate sums and products without prompting or support. When calculating sums and products, they check that their answers make sense, estimating answers mentally by rounding to single-digit multiples of 10.

## Level 5   Number Level Statements

### Cluster Level Description

Students read, write, say, and understand the meaning, order and relative magnitude of whole and decimal numbers, negative integers, fractions, straightforward ratios and percentages. These students understand the meaning, use and connections between the four operations on whole, decimal and fractional numbers to choose appropriate operations. They calculate with whole numbers, decimals using mostly mental strategies for whole numbers, money and readily visualised factions.

### Elaboration

#### Understand Whole and Decimal Numbers

Students who have achieved Level 5 move easily between various ways of representing numbers and quantities. They know that 'one quarter off' is the same as '25% off' and that, in each case, 0.75 of the original amount remains. Students have a sense of the relative size of such fractional quantities, saying, for example: *One third off is better than a 30% discount*.

These students know that the digits to the right of the decimal place have decreasing values in powers of 10, and say and read any decimal number. They order decimals, including when the number of places is unequal; for example, when finding a book in the library, they know that 6.7 comes after 6.175. Students understand the link between 0.35 as being $\frac{35}{100}$ and $\frac{3}{10} + \frac{5}{100}$ and can partition decimal numbers flexibly in multiple ways; for example, they know that 0.36 is 0.3 + 0.06 and also 0.2 + 0.16, and so on.

Students read a wide range of scales involving decimals, including where each calibration may not be labelled. They can also use ratios in straightforward ways; for example, to work out the quantities needed to make a 1-in-4 mixture of compost to soil, and they know that a 1-to-5 ratio would be less rich.

#### Understand Operations

Students use the inverse relationship between multiplication and division when dealing with situations involving scales, familiar rates, areas and combinations. They can use division in situations where the divisors are decimal and fractional numbers and may be bigger than the number being divided into. They know that multiplying and dividing can each have the effect of increasing or reducing the original quantity, depending on the size of the multiplier or the divisor, knowing, for example, that dividing by one third triples the amount.

Students at Level 5 are able to find a number or numbers that satisfy constraints, such as: 'What number am I if half of me, add 1, is 41?' and 'A square has an area of more than 100. What can you say about the length of its sides?' Students also find pairs of numbers that satisfy constraints. Thus, they list systematically all possible length/breadth pairs for rectangles made from exactly 36 squares.

**Calculate**

Students at Level 5 are skilled in mental computation with whole numbers and money. They calculate mentally with easily visualised fractions and record the stages in adding and subtracting fractions that they cannot complete mentally. These students use a range of efficient, though not necessarily standard, written methods to add, subtract, multiply and divide whole numbers and common and decimal fractions.

However, for multipliers and divisors of more than one digit, students may use a calculator. They use their calculators efficiently, including when dealing with fractions and percentages, and they sequence calculations to suit the conventions of their own calculators. These students estimate when it is sensible to do so, rather than making exact calculations unnecessarily. For example, when asked whether $30 is enough to purchase six of an item, which costs $4.88, they make a rough calculation by rounding $4.88 up to $5. At Level 5, students will be experimenting with short cuts for doing calculations. For instance, they might notice that six lots of $5 is exactly $30, but that for each $5, there is 12 cents more than the item cost. So, the change is 72 cents.

Pro Forma

Classroom Plan for Week ___, Term ___    Year Level: ___

| Outcome/Key Understanding | Mathematical Focus | Activities | Focus Questions | Observations/Anecdotes |
|---|---|---|---|---|
| | | | | |

175

# Bibliography

Carle, E. 2000, *The Very Hungry Caterpillar*, Hamilton, London.

Hutchins, P. 1986, *The Doorbell Rang*, Mulberry Books, New York.

McIntosh, A., De Nardi, E. and Swan, P. 1994, *Think Mathematically*, Longman Cheshire, Melbourne, Australia.

Nunes, T. and Bryant, P. 1996, *Children Doing Mathematics*, Blackwell Publishers Ltd. Oxford, UK.

Ross, S. H. February 1989, 'Parts, wholes and place value: a developmental view', *Arithmetic Teacher*, pp 48–49.

Swan, M. *The Meaning and Use of Decimals, Calculator-Based Diagnostic Tests and Teaching Materials* (pilot version), Shell Centre for Mathematical Education, University of Nottingham, UK.

y:

it

has

umber

are 5
of 15
ree

4
10 and

d 3

r
pcess
es as

n

ating,

## As students move from the Factoring phase to the Operating phase, they:

- often continue to rely largely on their knowledge of the 'named' places in reading and writing numbers, so have difficulty writing numbers with more than four digits
- may label the places to the right of the decimal point as tenths and hundredths and write 2.45 as $2 + \frac{4}{10} + \frac{5}{100}$, for example, but cannot link this with other ways of writing the decimal, such as: $2 + \frac{45}{100}$
- may think decimals with two places are always hundredths and write 2.45 as $2 + \frac{45}{100}$, but do not link this with the pattern in whole-number place value and so do not see 2.45 as $2 + \frac{4}{10} + \frac{5}{100}$
- often are unable to select a common partitioning (denominator) to enable two fractions to be compared or combined unless an equivalence they already know is involved
- often ignore the need to draw two fractions on identical wholes in order to compare or combine them
- may be unable to select an appropriate operation in situations where they cannot think of the multiplier or divisor as a whole number
- may resist selecting division where the required division involves dividing a number by a bigger number
- often believe that multiplication 'makes bigger' and division 'makes smaller'.

y:

r line
tern

l

nto

ke